From Fatherless

to

Fearless

Unstoppable Women Share Their Journeys of Tragedy and Triumph

CANDICE CREAR

FOREWORD BY CRYSTAL PERKINS

From Fatherless

to

Fearless

Unstoppable Women Share Their Journeys
of Tragedy and Triumph

*Vicki,
Thanks so much
for your support
stories to move books
that will impact the
generations to come. With love,
Jai*

CANDICE CREAR

FOREWORD BY CRYSTAL PERKINS

COPYRIGHT

Editor: Greta Barnes, Candice Crear, Tenita Johnson

Cover Design: Angie A.

ISBN: 978-0-9989306-4-0

LCCN: 2017919777

Printed in the United States of America

 # DEDICATION

To all the fatherless daughters, who are looking for examples on their journey, this book is for you.

Other Books by Candice Crear:

Invisible Dad
Invisible God, I'm Waiting

TABLE OF CONTENTS

ACKNOWLEDGMENTS

Giving all glory and honor to God, Whom provided the vision and provision to make this book come to fruition. To all of my anthology sisters who were vulnerable and bold enough to stand in their truth, I love and celebrate you.

 # FOREWORD

From Fatherless to Fearless is such a bold title. When one thinks of being fatherless, it often brings forth unwelcoming thoughts and feelings of sadness, brokenness and loneliness. Being fatherless is an epidemic today, and sadly, it has become somewhat normal for many families in the United States. The 2017 U.S. Census Bureau research shows that out of about 12 million single parent families with children under the age of 18, more than 80% are headed by single mothers. Among this percentage of single mothers: 45% of them are currently divorced or separated; 1.7% are widowed; and 34% have never been married. Having a Bachelor's Degree in Social Work and a Master's in Counseling increases my awareness of how this epidemic affects one during childhood to adulthood, causing problems that include, but are not limited to: behavioral issues, depression, suicide, low self-esteem, fear of abandonment and rejection.

Given the assignment from God to write this foreword pushed me in many ways. Not only did it allow me to support the author, Candice, and her vision, but it enabled me to open up and discuss memories of my childhood. It gave me the opportunity to share parts of my testimony that have yet to be revealed. It also reminded me of how healing from fatherlessness gave me a sense of courage, strength, leadership, humility and purpose, and the will to be *fearless*.

I don't have many memories, as it relates to the relationship between my mother and father. My mother and father split when I was six years old. My mom would take me to my father's house on Fridays after school, and I stayed with him until Sunday afternoons after church. I have fun memories of cooking with him in the mornings and enjoying the outdoors each weekend. But the older I got, the more I observed my parents arguing, which rarely happened. I noticed a lack of financial commitment from my father and fewer weekend visits over time.

My father was a loving, kind, hard-working guy. But, before long, I found out that he was also a *drug addict*. I have many sad memories of being fatherless due to my father's addiction. However, one thing remained: he was still Daddy and he deserved the utmost respect. Inside, I was hurt, abandoned, sad and hopeless. But no matter what, he was still my father. As I look back on my childhood, I remember my greatest desire during my studies and my career was to help one person: my father. My desire to help him pushed me and inspired me more than words can express. No matter how old I grew, I always had the excitement of seeing and talking to Daddy. I was always that little thrilled girl. I looked forward to seeing him, just like I had on Fridays when I was six years old.

All I wanted was for him to get better. But, unfortunately, I couldn't see it come to fruition. While in graduate school, my father was diagnosed with lung cancer. He passed away a short time later with me by his side. I often tell people that my father's *death* gave me *life*. Throughout his life and illness, I remained hopeful. I prayed more than I ever had. My faith continued to grow. I was stretched and tested like never before. Through God, I healed from my past and learned how to live without worry or fear.

Like the fearless women in this book, being fatherless gave me a sense of drive and ambition, and allowed God to direct my path according to His purpose. I commend both Candice and the co-authors in this book for having the faith and tenacity to share their stories of navigating the fatherless epidemic. Although each chapter is unique, they all lead to embracing the journey of fearlessness. It is my prayer that this book will inspire women worldwide to move *From Fatherless to Fearless*. This book is life-changing. Be encouraged and may God bless you!

Candice, thank you again for your courage to birth such an inspiring book. I look forward to witnessing all that God has in store because of your obedience. May God continue to bless you!

Love, Crystal Perkins

Chapter 1

Missing Pieces of the Puzzle

Kimberlee Hensley

"For I know the plans I have for you," declares the Lord, "plans to prosper you and not to harm you, plans to give you hope and a future."

Jeremiah 29:11, New International Version

At six years old, I experienced my first heartbreak. I was playing outside with two of the neighbor's kids on a warm, sunny day. All seemed to be going well. That's until they started teasing me saying, "You're adopted! You're adopted!"

My simple reply was, "No I'm not."

But, it wasn't enough to stop them from speaking those words. I went inside the house and told my mother what the boys said. Her response caused a bit of confusion because she didn't say I *wasn't* adopted.

In fact, her reply was, "Do you know what that means?"

I said, "Yes," convinced that whatever it was, I *wasn't*. She then explained to me that sometimes a mommy and a daddy have a baby that they are unable to care for, so they give the baby to another mommy and daddy who can. I stared into her eyes, but spoke no words. My heart was set that this was not my truth.

She then said the words that crushed my spirit, "You *are* adopted."

I felt deceived by the two people I had trusted the most. I was embarrassed because I was determined to prove the two boys wrong, but they knew a life-changing truth about me before I did. How could my parents keep this from me? *Why* would they keep this from me? I was heartbroken and confused, but I believed the safest thing to do was to keep my feelings and questions to myself. I doubted their credibility. That was the beginning of a journey that had many highs and lows, twists and turns.

As I saw a woman approaching us with a small boy and a baby girl, my face blushed.

I was raised as an only child, and I was the apple of my parents' eyes. Although I was treated like a princess, what my heart longed for was a brother or sister, someone I could play with, take baths with, share bedtime stories with—just like in the movies. But, my mother was unable to carry a child. She would conceive and miscarry, pregnancy after pregnancy. So, when my mother shared the good news that I had brothers and sisters, I was elated!

We took a ride into town and parked at an apartment complex. As I saw a woman approaching us with a small boy and a baby girl, my face blushed. I wanted to hold them, kiss them and keep them because they were mine! I finally had what my heart desired for so long. After a short visit, I experienced my second heartbreak. I left those apartments and my siblings stayed. I sat in the back seat, staring at a picture of my little brother, baby sister and the woman who turned out to be my biological mother.

Since my heart was consumed with love for my two younger siblings, I didn't initially put too much thought into the woman that was present, nor the absence of a man that would have completed the equation. Every night, alone in my room, I held that picture, hoping to see my little brother and baby sister again. Days, weeks and months passed by. Just when my eagerness to see them began to disappear, I had an encounter with a man I was unfamiliar with. I was riding my bike and went further away from my home than I was allowed. I was on an adventure to pick berries from the neighbor's tree. As I looked around to make sure my parents didn't know I had wandered so far from our house, I noticed a man on the road watching me, looking at me as if he knew me. I rushed home through all the neighbors' yards to tell my mom about the man. She assured me he was a stranger and reminded me not to go that far from home again.

That night, as I looked down at the picture, questions came to my mind. *Where is the father? Who is he? Why is he not in the picture?* My hope was to find my birth certificate because I was certain the name of my father would

I noticed a man on the road watching me.

be on there. I suddenly had an urge to piece together this family, because it was a part of the puzzle of who I was. I took it upon myself to search through my mother's important documents because I doubted she would share this information with me willingly. I came across an old, worn out piece of paper that seemed to be just what I needed. But as I examined the paper, the only male name that I didn't recognize was the doctor that signed it. I felt defeated. I neatly put all the papers back how I found them.

It was seven years later when I got to see that precious round face of my baby sister again. I was 13 and had my first teen crush. The two of us met at a local playground. As we were having a conversation, I caught a glimpse of a little girl who caused me to blush in the same way I experienced blushing at those apartments.

I said to my teen crush, "I think that's my sister." He suggested that I talk to her. Overwhelmed with a variety of emotions, I decided to approach her.

"Are you Kara?" I asked.

When she replied, "Yes," it was difficult for me to process that after all of these years, my baby sister was right in front of me. It had been so long that I didn't know exactly what words to say.

I mumbled, "I'm Kim, your sister." Immediately, she invited me to her home. I wanted to spend as much time with her as possible, so I didn't hesitate to walk a couple of blocks to a house that had the key to unlock the answers to my questions.

He's black and I'm white.

Shortly after we arrived, my biological mother asked if I wanted to meet my dad. I was completely caught off guard because I didn't even think it was an option. Until this moment, I knew nothing about my biological father. Once I agreed, she made a phone call and, moments later, a red car pulled up. A tall, muscular, brown-skinned man stepped out. My thoughts were, *"That can't be him. He's black and I'm white. He is so tall and handsome. There must be a mistake."* I didn't outwardly express my denial because, inwardly, I hoped he was truly my father. I wanted another piece to the puzzle. Our conversation was brief. I was awkward, but he seemed relaxed. After answering his questions about how my grades were in school and what sports I played, I quickly returned to the park. I didn't share the experience with my adoptive parents because I was concerned they wouldn't allow me to return. I feared the consequences of them knowing I met the man they didn't reveal to me.

From Kindergarten until late elementary school, my family moved frequently and I didn't understand why. In the middle of fourth grade, my parents decided to move from Ohio to Illinois. When we settled in, I quickly developed new friends that welcomed me into their church routine. That summer, I attended my first Christian camp. One evening, while most of the kids were in the gymnasium, I sat on the floor, listening intently to the leaders share their testimonies about Jesus. I had heard the message before, but I viewed it as a way of life for the perfect families with white picket fences. I didn't think it was an offer meant for me, the girl who was adopted and separated from her siblings. The girl who didn't have a steady home and changed schools every year. As I continued to listen to the leaders, it felt different this time. It didn't just sound like a fairytale; it felt like something very present, something that could be possible for me. Did Jesus love *me* that much that He would die for me? After all, my biological parents let me go and my adoptive parents didn't care enough to keep me in a stable home. My heart filled with hope that Jesus really did love me, and that He always would if I trusted Him. As my eyes filled with tears, I told Jesus that I needed Him. I told him I trusted Him and I wanted Him to be with me, no matter where I go.

One year later, my parents moved us back to Ohio, promising it would be the last time they would uproot me. Soon, one of my friends welcomed me to attend her church. Going regularly, I learned what was expected of me as a Christian. So, when the opportunity to be baptized was presented, I knew it was something I wanted to do. I was so determined to live this Christian life and do things exactly how God intended. Life was going great. I attended the same school for three years. My best friend and I had sleepovers regularly and discussed our dreams of being missionaries in other countries.

I started a new journey with my biological family.

When I became confident of my routine, my parents revealed they were planning to move back to Illinois. I was now 14 and believed I was old enough to make decisions about my life. So, I suggested that I live with my biological mother. I wanted to remain at the same school. Once my biological mother and adoptive parents agreed to the request, I started a new journey with my biological family.

I saw this as an opportunity to confirm that this brown-skinned man I met a year prior, and hadn't seen since, was indeed my father. I was also able to meet my other siblings. This was an adventure that I wasn't sure if I was prepared for, but I was ecstatic to experience! It was complicated getting to know all of my siblings because there were nine altogether, who had been raised in five different homes. My biological father immediately took on the role of a dad, picking me up after school for dinner, taking me shopping and providing money for necessities. I still wondered if it was true that he was my father.

During one of our evenings together, he told me that I was wrongfully taken from him. He said he tried to fight for me for a long time, but to no avail. It felt really good to hear, but because of how the adoption was revealed, I didn't completely believe that to be true. He also shared a story about a day he was driving down a country road and saw a little girl. The second I engaged in eye contact, and gave a quick smile, he was certain it was me. When he received the information of what house I lived in, he came back to knock on the door, and the house was empty. This was confirmation that the unfamiliar man on the road was not a stranger; he was my biological father who had been searching for me!

I wanted to hear the stories of me as a baby, how the adoption happened, and his attempts to search for me during my childhood. He showed me court papers and pictures, and shared stories that I vaguely remembered. I soon understood that when my biological mother could not take care of me, the courts were not in favor of a brown-skinned man raising a white-skinned baby. This was the first time I formally understood the devastation of racial discrimination. It had redirected my whole life, unbeknownst to me. I came to terms with who I was. My mind was now in agreement with what my heart had hoped for: to find the missing pieces of the puzzle of my identity.

All Things Work Together

"And we know that in all things God works for the good of those who love him, who have been called according to his purpose."

Romans 8:28, New International Version

My heart's focus quickly became redirected at the age of 15, when my pre-teen crush asked me to be his high school sweetheart. We spent an abundance of time together, and I mistakenly took lust for love. I was consumed with our relationship and started participating in activities

I knew were sinful. I felt the need to hide from God, so I put aside my relationship with Him and put my trust and focus on my boyfriend. For seven years, I turned away from church, prayer and reading the Bible. My heart longed to be involved, but my mind was convinced that I needed to be married before returning to God. My boyfriend didn't even want to discuss marriage. I was depressed and suffered from anxiety. I learned a hard lesson.

When we choose to do what we know is wrong, the consequences that follow are painful.

When we choose to do what we know is wrong, the consequences that follow are painful. I drank alcohol and partied as often as possible, but I continued to feel unsatisfied. I eventually decided that ending the relationship would bring me happiness. I was young, single, independent and still loved to party. I expected to feel complete. But, that didn't happen.

A few months after the breakup, a coworker invited me to her church. Since I was no longer living with a man I wasn't married to, I accepted the invitation. When I arrived at Phillips Temple Church, I was greeted with hugs. I felt the sincere worship of Jesus through the choir, received the Word of God directly from the Bible, and spent multiple times in heartfelt prayer. I knew, without a doubt, this was where I needed to be. Slowly, my life began to transform. I limited my partying to Friday nights so I could get in bed early on Saturday nights and be well-rested for church service on Sunday mornings. I removed the worldly behaviors that I had grown accustomed to because I wanted more of the truth. This love and growth I experienced was so much more rewarding than a night of drunkenness and a hangover. When I fell again, Jesus was there to catch me. He'd continuously remind me that He was there to teach me.

As a child, my adoptive father wiped my tears when I scraped my knee or got lectured by my mother. But, I didn't trust him with the tears that flowed from heartache. As a teen, my biological father took the initiative to talk with me, but I wouldn't share in depth the thoughts or feelings I was experiencing because I knew he wasn't fond of my upbringing. I wanted to have closeness and open communication with the both of them, but I couldn't. I doubted my adoptive father would be completely honest, and I feared my biological father would respond unpleasantly.

While experiencing this new-found daddy-daughter relationship, I allowed myself to be vulnerable. I had to trust and not be afraid. I spoke to my heavenly Father in the way I desired to speak to my earthly fathers. While doing this, He showed me that He is my protection, my guidance and my encouragement. When I expressed my heartache, disappointments, childhood stories, dreams, doubts and fears, He let me know that it was all for a reason and a purpose. In those moments of vulnerability, I was reminded that love conquers all, and that I am to forgive, just as I have been forgiven by the Father. I didn't know the purpose of everything I had been through (or was going through) at the time, but I *did* know that if I continued to trust Him,

I chose to forgive all of my parents, and myself, so I could love them in the way Jesus loved me – unconditionally.

11

and remained obedient to what He asked of me, He would reveal it to me. I chose to forgive all of my parents, and myself, so I could love them in the way Jesus loved me – *unconditionally.*

Trust in the Lord

"So in Christ Jesus you are all children of God through faith."

Galatians 3:26, New International Version

In October 2014, my pastor shared that the church was forming a missionary team and traveling to India. I thought it sounded nice, but I left it at that. A month later, my pastor approached me and said, "Kim, I want you to pray about going on the mission trip to India." As I prayed over the trip, the Holy Spirit reminded me of the conversations my best friend and I had as young girls during our sleepovers and our dreams of being missionaries in other countries. I felt this trip was something God wanted me to do. I acknowledged that if it was His will, He would work it all out. Each time a worry or concern came to mind, I whispered, "I trust you Lord." Step by step, it came together—the passport, the immunizations and the visa approval. My vacation request was accepted. Family took on the responsibilities of my children. I received financial support. I also received confirmation of protection. Soon, I was on a flight to another continent! I knew going was in God's will, but I was uncertain of my purpose.

When we arrived in India that Sunday, we attended a church service and their pastor asked us to conduct intercessory prayer. I was hesitant, but I understood the importance of being obedient. After I prayed for a young lady, she expressed her gratitude and said it was exactly what she needed. Days into the trip, we had a meeting with a group of girls who were rescued from the sex slave trade. Immediately, my eyes caught the eyes of the same young lady I had prayed for. We bonded right away. At that moment, I knew God had sent me there for her, one of His daughters that was so precious to Him. He used my childhood experiences to relate to her so she would feel comfortable enough to let down her guard and receive the word God had for her. My purpose was to be the vessel, a *true* messenger. That trip was life-changing. It confirmed I was to be a missionary.

I am grateful to say that both my biological and adoptive family have remained in my life. I have a unique relationship with each one of my siblings, and they all have their own special place in my heart. I have found beauty in the range of skin tones we each have, and I am confident in who I am. God has faithfully revealed to me the purpose of the pain. I was adopted, so now I can relate to those who have been abandoned. Growing up without my siblings means that I know what it feels like for someone to long for their brother and/or sister. Moving

I am fulfilling my purpose as God has chosen me to be a worker in His harvest.

frequently resulted in traveling without fear of the unknown and the ability to engage in conversations with strangers. The attempt to fill a void with lust and partying enabled me to show the same patience for others that God had for me.

I am fulfilling my purpose as God has chosen me to be a worker in His harvest. I have been on the mission field three times, remaining obedient to where I am called to go. The pain and healing has equipped me to share the Gospel so that God's children are able to answer the questions others often can't answer for them: *Where is my father? Who is he? Why is he not in the picture?* I am able to share that the *good news* is not too good to be true because I've experienced it myself. You, too, can call God by His name; Father, Daddy, Abba!

For more information about Kimberlee and her fearless way of life, visit www.KimberleeDanielle.com.

SELF-REFLECTION QUESTIONS

1. What steps noted in Kimberlee's journey could you use to walk in healing?

    _____

    _____

    _____

    _____

    _____

    _____

    _____

2. What experiences in your life have you had that God could use you to help others in a similar situation?

    _____

    _____

    _____

    _____

    _____

    _____

    _____

SELF-REFLECTION QUESTIONS

3. Have there been words spoken to you that you believe may have been from God, but you aren't certain? What can you do to determine if those words were a message from God?

_____

_____

_____

_____

_____

_____

4. Is there something God has placed on your heart to do that you have not focused on? What can you do to move forward?

_____

_____

_____

_____

_____

_____

Financially Full, Emotionally Empty

Tanya Cooper

"My old self has been crucified with Christ. It is no longer I who live, but Christ lives in me. So I live in this earthly body by trusting in the Son of God, who loved me and gave himself for me."

Galatians 2:20, New Living Translation

My father's house was beautiful. Victorian-style, with huge grandfather clocks and European rugs. I remember the huge bay windows that overlooked the lake in our backyard. I had over three thousand square feet to run around in. The grass was a beautiful green and always stayed well-manicured throughout the years. The weather in Florida was flawless in every way. This gated community had a good school district and palm trees everywhere. Then, *he'd* come home. The champagne-colored Acura would pull up and park, and the door would open. It was my dad. He was always well-dressed and handsome. He'd walk right toward me as I waited with a smile. From there, he'd walk right past me, as if I didn't exist. No

He'd walk right past me, as if I didn't exist.

smile. No hug. He wouldn't even say my name. I felt empty and rejected. I remember the cold neglect vividly.

As a child, I suffered from severe double ear infections that caused doctors to consider placing tubes in my ears to alleviate the pain. I screamed in excruciating agony any time I had an infection. One day, my dad came into the room. I didn't stretch my arms toward him because I was holding my ears. The tears blurred my vision as my dad picked me up high. He violently shook me back and forth while screaming, "Shut that noise up! I said shut that noise up!" Somewhere, hidden deep in the background, my mother watched. When my father eventually dropped me on the couch and left, my mom came in quietly and put my face in her chest to muffle my screams. I learned from that point on to take pain silently. I learned how to cry inwardly.

As time went on, I yearned for my father's attention. I wanted him to notice me, but all he did was criticize my weight, how I dressed, my skin and the way I fixed my hair. Either he was criticizing me, or I didn't exist to him at all. We could be in the same room and he would completely ignore me. Silence became the loudest noise. Even though he was physically there, we were miles apart. Then, he'd walk away from me. My dad was the first man I ever loved. He was also the first man who broke my heart.

My family was perfect on the outside. But, on the inside, the house was filled with absolute chaos and abuse. One night, I woke up to my mom screaming. I got up and went down the hall just enough to see what was going on. My dad was punching my mother repeatedly. My mother's blood and tears streamed down her face. I was frozen. Stiff. Fear, swelling to a crescendo, paralyzed my entire body. I was useless and just as helpless as my mother. My father finally stopped and walked away, leaving my mother on the floor. He soon converted the physical abuse to a verbal form as he was walking out the door. My mom would scream and cry, but she always went back to the illusion of being a happy wife, like the ones on TV. To the world, my father was a great provider and the perfect man. But to me, the financial stability was all he provided. I never knew what it was like to experience lack because my father was an amazing provider. He took care of everything, which allowed my mother to be a stay-at-home wife, and for both my sister and I to attend private schools. I never had to wear the same clothes twice in a month, but that wasn't enough.

Proverbs 22:6 tells us to train our children in the way that they should go so that when they are mature, they will continue in that proper way. But, what happens when your parents don't? My father taught me to react with anger and violence. He taught me to ignore others' feelings. He also raised me to be as brutal as possible with my words. He raised me to abuse the ones I love and to block out anyone who got too close. Subconsciously, I picked up the lifestyle of my mom, as well. She taught me to accept the disrespect and brutality of men. Although my father was physically there, his love, care, comfort, warmth and attention were invisible and intangible.

In front of friends, my family was an illusion. Truth be told, all of our dynamics were built upon dysfunction, and I was on my way to carry out our legacy. When a young girl is neglected by the father she loves, she tends to embrace the attention of boys, believing that she'll find that love in them. Of course, I was no different. I started having sex at fifteen and got pregnant the very next year. My father put me out of his house and sent me to live with relatives. He

When a young girl is neglected by the father she loves, she tends to embrace the attention of boys.

kept my child, which caused a relational disconnection between my son and me. I had no job, nowhere to go, and no idea what to do.

Even though I was no longer with my dad, his words and ways toward me never left. I rehearsed his criticism in my mind. I was conditioned to think about myself, and even treat myself in the ways in which he did. This kept me empty inside, so I started stripping. I longed for the attention, and I really needed the money. The lifestyle of a stripper exposes a woman to multitudes of perverted men. Brutal men. Lusting men. These ungodly men had a lot of money. From bankers to drug lords, all of these men focused on the flesh of a woman, with no concern about her spirit or mind. This was the case for me, too, for quite some time.

Then one day, while in the strip club, a man approached me who recognized the little girl in me. He was fourteen years my senior. His conversation was different from the conversations of the other men who approached me. I wasn't used to this type of treatment. He was kind to me and concerned about my future. I fell in love and got married. Soon after, I was pregnant for a second time. But, it wasn't a fairytale marriage. We had our share of disagreements, like all married couples. I coped with those disagreements in the same way in which my dad did. I became brutal. At times, I attacked my husband physically because that was the only response I had for settling disputes. I was my father's daughter, and his ways were ingrained within me. We stayed together for six years. Under the circumstances, that was the best we could do.

After divorcing my husband, I continued to delve into one abusive relationship after another. When a broken woman deals with broken men, they function in what they think is love, but it truly isn't. By this time, I was finally able to get my own place. Thanks to my mother's help, I had a roof over my head and it was all my own. But a roof over one's head doesn't heal a broken mind. I was still empty inside, looking for a love that would fill my void. I bought a whole new wardrobe and wore new hairstyles. I also bought furniture for the house. I was trying to recreate myself, but this new creation continued to attract the wrong type of men. I thought love was found in the finer things in life, but fancy hotels, restaurants and large houses could not heal the pain of this magnitude.

My depression was at an all-time high. I was taking several medications, which caused me to stay in bed all day long. One day, while lying in the bed and overcome with depression, I heard a very small, still voice say, "You're dying." The devil used the brokenness of my father's treatment to keep me in a lifestyle of confusion and destruction. If the enemy sees that you're resisting him in one way, he'll try to tempt you in other ways. So, I was falling for the same tricks. My father wasn't a church-going man. He never taught me the ways of God. The attributes of a true godly man were alien to me. My father's neglect in raising me properly continued to bear its burden in my life. I was blind and had no discernment.

You're dying.

Facing Forgiveness

"Put on the whole armor of God, that ye may be able to stand against the wiles of the devil."

Ephesians 6:11, King James Version

The effects of my father being emotionally unavailable lasted from age 16 to 35. What I realized is, that without Christ, a woman will not come out of her dark place. She will remain in that condition for the rest of her life. The journey to freedom was a process. I had to see myself as God sees me. I was used to rejection and I didn't know where to begin to heal.

I committed to a church home and become active in ministry. From my experiences, I saw how generational curses started. I had to die to my flesh because my fleshly mindset was generationally cursed.

I had associated love with money for so long that I truly thought they went hand-in-hand. I started having sex with men because they were either giving me money, buying me things, or telling me the things I longed to hear from my father. The little girl in me longed to hear, "I love you" from him. Reading God's Word taught me to forgive. So, I decided to apply forgiveness to the most difficult issues of my life. The unwanted emotions became a part of who I was. I didn't realize I was nurturing my pain, since it was the one thing that I had total control over—so I thought. As my birthday approached, I decided to write a letter to my father to express my feelings and release him from any unforgiveness I still held in my heart. This lifted a heavy weight off my shoulders.

When you walk around with unforgiveness and bitterness, you open yourself up to sickness and infirmities. I realized that the only way God's love was going to be able to penetrate my life was for me to let go of the hurt my father caused me. Letting go was not easy; in fact, it was one of the hardest things I had to do. I experienced God working *in* me and *through* me once I surrendered. Many times, I could be driving in my car and go into prayer—not because I wanted to—but because God was the operator of the car (my body) and I was just the passenger. I prayed for people who

I didn't understand it right then, but I was in a purging process.

24

hurt me and for those who had forsaken me. With tears rolling down my face, I'd scream and pray out loud. I couldn't believe the words that were coming out of my mouth. I had no control over them. At that moment, I started to feel different. Since then, my life has never been the same. I'm happier and there is a joy in me that can't be taken away. God's agape love has replaced every broken area of my life.

So, I asked God, "What do I do now?" The spirit of God spoke to me and said, "Live for me. Share everything you have been through with people who are willing to listen." Then, everything made sense. Through all the trials, and feelings of hurt and rejection, God was with me the whole time. My life was different. I was no longer *fatherless*. God is my father, and I just needed to embrace Him. I rejected Him because of my ignorance. From that point on, I led many women to salvation. They were broken, just like I once was. I vowed to become the same voice to others that I previously needed for myself. God made me fearless in that I was able to face my greatest issue—forgiving an invisible father. I am no longer ashamed of my story because God has used it to help other women. You shouldn't be ashamed of your story, either. It will inspire others.

"Praise be to the God and Father of our Lord Jesus Christ, the Father of compassion and the God of all comfort, who comforts us in all our troubles, so that we can comfort those in any trouble with the comfort we ourselves receive from God."

2 Corinthians 1:3-4, New International Version

We have to see the power of God in all that we go through, even though we don't like some of the things that have happened to us. The Lord, Jesus Christ, is the answer to everything. Cast all your cares (issues, problems, dilemmas, doubts, worries, troubles and mistakes) on God. Go straight to God in order to find rest for your soul. Come out of a worldly mindset and receive the mind that God wants you to have. He can truly fix it all. We need to have a Father who will never leave us nor forsake us. We need to have a Father who will never emotionally abandon us. We need to have a Father who continually gives us everything that we need.

Smiling Again

"She is clothed with strength and dignity, and she laughs without fear of the future. When she speaks, her words are wise, and she gives instruction with kindness."

Proverbs 31:25-26, New Living Translation

God is so good! I just can't tell you how good He is! It's funny how God can totally transform your life in ways you've never dreamed of. After years of torn, broken and damaged relationships, God has blessed me with a wonderful godly husband. Being with him hasn't always been easy because I had to work at accepting his love. My husband is different from any other man I have ever known. Fear almost caused me to miss out on my blessing. It got to the point where I

Fear almost caused me to miss out on my blessing.

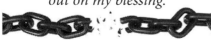

said to myself, "I'm scared, God, and I don't trust my own decisions. But I'm trusting you. Because of that, I'm going to walk straight into this marriage, fearless and in faith." My husband reminded me daily that I was going to have to get used to being loved by him. He always reminds me that he was prepared for this life's journey with me, and that it would take time for me to heal. My husband helped me come out of a mindset of doubt and fear.

Through His fatherly love, God removes all fear. Through His love, God has given me peace, joy and comfort. I see the beauty in everything now, and it's not hard to smile anymore. The joy of being alive comes naturally. From my God-given inner peace, I now know it's not a matter of *if* things are going to be alright; it may be a matter of time, but things *are* going to be alright. I know who my Father is now. My Father is God, who rules and reigns in Heaven! Being aware of God's love for me has made me bold. I know who I am! When I minister to others, I go casually with my bright tattoos showing, letting God direct me to those I need to approach. I've ministered to single moms, prostitutes, drug dealers and more. About once a month, I visit Atlanta and go to strip clubs to minister to the women. I've had a club owner offer me a job, to which I answered, "I work for the Lord now." I'm not moved by what I see because I know the consequences.

One time, I approached a stripper who reminded me of myself. I offered her money to sit and talk with me. She was very guarded at first, but she eventually felt comfortable talking to me about being abandoned by her father. She even spoke of how it affected her over the years and that her own child was being raised without a father. I told her that when I looked at her, I didn't see her mistakes or her current situation. I told her that I saw the godly queen she was destined to become. Tears ran down her face as she asked me why she continued to pick the wrong men. I told her that until she forgives her father, she'd continue to accept men that are just like him. It's pretty amazing that while ministering to others, I run into the old me often. I know just what to say to every woman I run into because they are exactly where I used to be.

There are so many broken women who need help. As I minister, some listen; but there are also those who won't. However, I know that I am planting a seed in every woman I come in contact with. I know the root of their deepest issues stem from being fatherless. I'll continue to share my testimony with these women. I'm comfortable talking to anyone now because I know that my Father is forever with me. I no longer fight with my hands or hurtful words. I fight with the gifts God placed within me when He formed me in my mother's womb. Now that I know who I am (and whose I am), the enemy intensifies his attacks by continuously bringing up my past. But my Heavenly Father always reminds me, "Tanya, there is work to be done."

Doing His work is different for everyone. That is why I am now the founder of *HolyFit!*, a motivational support group for women. *HolyFit!* is an exercise ministry that helps women let go of the extra weight in life. We work out at the gym to get rid of the extra physical weight, while also ministering to each other to get rid of the extra weight of

Now this diamond shines brighter than ever!

28

unhealthy mental and spiritual lifestyles. I see now that when I step into a room, God steps into that room with me. That's my mindset. That's my way. My presence changes the atmosphere! I've learned that you never know who you'll cross paths with during your day or whose life you may impact along the way. A person wouldn't think that I've been through half of what I've been through because my character no longer reflects my past. My father in Heaven has purified me in the furnace of affliction. Now this diamond shines brighter than ever! My advice to you is to speak life to yourself and to others, and life will surely be added unto you!

"To know me is to love me. I live my life in color. Nothing is ever just black and white."

Tanya Cooper

For more information about Tanya and her fearless way of life, visit www.TanyaLanayCooper.com.

SELF-REFLECTION QUESTIONS

1. Why is forgiveness important?

   _____

   _____

   _____

   _____

   _____

   _____

   _____

2. Explain a time when you were fearful, but because of your faith, you became fearless.

   _____

   _____

   _____

   _____

   _____

   _____

   _____

SELF-REFLECTION QUESTIONS

3. Have you ever associated love with money? If so, why?

_____

_____

_____

_____

_____

_____

4. Has there been a time when you financially had everything, but you were emotionally empty? If so, how did that make you feel?

_____

_____

_____

_____

_____

_____

_____

Chapter 3

Take Me with You

Daunita Saunders

*"When my father and my mother forsake me, then the Lord
will take me up."*

Psalm 27:10, King James Version

I looked out the window many times, wondering if my daddy was coming to get me. It was an exciting day for me. It was my birthday. I just knew he would come. But he didn't. Things had changed, and I couldn't quite understand why. Everything was going just fine in the beginning. I was young and carefree. My mom took us to church so that we would have the foundation of Jesus Christ. Although my father didn't live with us, he came to visit. I loved my dad so much. I was a daddy's girl. When I was four years old, I had the chickenpox. I was so miserable. I woke up from a nap and I heard a familiar voice downstairs. I went to see who it was and my heart jumped with joy when I saw it was my father! I was ecstatic just knowing that he came to be with me while I was sick. He rubbed the calamine lotion on my skin to help me stop itching. He stayed for a while, but when he got ready to leave, I clung to him tight. I pleaded, "Take me with you!" I never wanted to let him go.

When I was a little girl, I pretended to read a book about a family that lived on the moon. They were the same color as the moon and looked like fluffy, rounded marshmallows. The father in the story was my father, the mother was my mother, and the sister and brother were my siblings. When the father hugged the child, that was my father hugging me. When he picked the child up and held her, that was me. Whenever I started missing my dad, I would look up to the moon at night and picture my father with a big smile on his face. I'd wonder what he was doing, if he missed me.

When I turned six years old, my life turned upside down. We lived downtown in a townhouse for four years, but it was time for a change. My mother decided to move us to a better community with better housing and

We moved about 30 minutes away, but in his eyes, it was as if we moved to Europe.

better schools. From that day forward, he became a full-time telephone dad. We moved about 30 minutes away, but in his eyes, it was as if we moved to Europe. He always made excuses as to why I couldn't spend time with him on the weekends. Whether it was, "I have to work" or "Wait until it gets cold" or "Wait until it warms up," there was always a reason why I couldn't see him. One Christmas, my dad bought me a Cabbage Patch Kid big wheel—at least I thought he did. That was one of my favorite Christmas moments. I was used to my mom purchasing me presents, but when my dad did, it was extra special. I felt joy inside like, "Wow! He didn't forget about me!" Although the presents were nice, for some reason, he was never there on Christmas morning when I opened them.

Going to church was a relief for me. I truly enjoyed getting to know other believers. I first gave my life to Christ and received the Holy Spirit when I was 15 years old. That was the happiest day of my life. Throughout all my experiences I've endured, there's nothing that compares to that day. My family attended church less and less. The day we stopped going is the day I was starving for hope.

With my dad no longer around, my life was slowly going downhill. He was easier to deal with when I was young, but things changed as I got older. Being on the phone with him was worse than talking to him in person. He was angry, mad – mad at the world, mad at my mom, and mad at us. The older I got, the more talking to him left me in tears and feeling down. Everything I did was wrong, and everything I did *not do* was wrong. I was often scared that I would say the wrong thing to him and set him off. Or I was scared I'd get yelled at for taking too long to answer him or call him back. So, talking to him was a gamble. I stopped returning his calls because I didn't feel like going through the emotional turmoil all the time.

Everything set him off, and I never knew how to really talk to him without him getting mad. I got sick of it, so I started arguing a little bit with him as I reached my teenage years. After the blowups, I'd end up being the one in tears. Then, we'd go a long time without speaking. If I didn't call him, he didn't call me. With both of us being too stubborn to call each other first, we grew further and further apart. Although he was the adult, we often switched roles. It's tough trying to be an adult when you're just an adolescent. I felt like I practically was begging him to be my dad.

I lived in Blue Ash for thirteen years and my father only traveled 30 minutes to see me four times. The last time was to pick me up to take me to get glasses in eighth grade. Then, he dropped me back off at home. The weird part about that outing with my daddy was coming back home and having my friends ask me, "Who took you to get your glasses?" To be able to say, "My daddy did!" felt so good inside. My friends were actually shocked because they hardly ever heard me talk about my daddy. They thought he was not in my life at all. They often heard me call their dads "Dad." I often wished their dads were mine. Here's a poem I wrote about my father when I was 17 years old:

Is He Coming to Get Me?

I looked out my window and up the street

To see if he was coming back for me.

The streets were empty, the rocks stood still;

I was about to give up on him, until…

I saw a car coming up the street.

It was grey. It was long, and it had my heart jumping beats.

I was happy, so happy that it might be him.

Then all of a sudden, my happiness dimmed.

Tears started falling out of my eyes.

I wanted to question the Lord and ask, "Why?"

Why do I have to go through all of this mess?

I am way too young to have all this stress.

I have forgiven him for all he has done.

My life without him will not be fun.

I remember when I was little when he stood by my side;

When I had chickenpox, and I cried and cried.

But years have gone by and we've moved away.

But I know he will come running back some day.

"Wait!" Another car is now coming past.

I thought it was him, but he flew by too fast.

Well, that gives me another reason to fear

That I will go through this exact same situation next year.

The Seed I Planted

"He brought me up also out of an horrible pit, out of the miry clay, and set my feet upon a rock, and established my goings."

Psalm 40:2, King James Version

I was 24 years old when my life took another drastic turn. I was pregnant. My father was so upset and treated me like I was a child. He failed to realize that I was an adult now and I was free to make my own choices. Trying to be a *real* father was not an option. He thought paying child support was enough to raise me all these years, but I truly needed him by my side. This turned out to be the biggest argument we ever had and the longest time we ever went without speaking to each other. I told myself I was done with him. I finally gave up on having a relationship with my dad.

He thought paying child support was enough to raise me all these years.

One day, I received the most disturbing phone call. My aunt was murdered. The shock and the devastation sent me into early labor that next morning. I was terrified. I had my baby boy, but not without complications. I ended up having what the doctors called post-partum depression. I was willing to give back my child in order to have my aunt back. After being told so many times after my aunt passed away, that when three new lives enter into the world, one has to go, all I did was feel guilty for my aunt not being here anymore. Maybe it was petty of me, but I was vulnerable at the time. When you're vulnerable, that is the best time for the devil to step right in and whisper deceitful little thoughts. I was fighting to heal, yet fighting to be a mother simultaneously.

To top it off, I was in a mentally abusive relationship. Although I ended the relationship in hopes of easing the pain, I would end up falling for another abusive man. Little did I know, I would be raped by him. My depression, coupled with his chaos, made for a dynamic no one wanted to see. The stronghold wouldn't allow me to get away from this guy. And although God gave me plenty of opportunities, I ended up right back in that same situation. While going on that roller coaster ride in that relationship, God let me know He was still there. He was just waiting on me to say, "Enough is enough." He was waiting on me to realize I needed His help, but I was lost. I didn't know how to move forward. Before I'd return back to God, death would strike again. This time, I lost a dear friend who was diagnosed with cancer and became very sick. She was my inspiration to be a Christian woman. At 2 a.m., I watched her take her last breath.

As time went on, I thought about my dad, but death would not leave me alone. That same year, I experienced the loss of my son's father. How do you tell a two-year-old his father is gone and that he will never see him again? How was I supposed to answer questions when he was old enough to start asking them? The saddest part was watching my son slowly forget who his dad was. Only God could give me the real strength I needed to go through all that pain. I continued to go through trials and tribulations, but by 2012, I was running back to Jesus. I gave my life back to Christ, and I've been living in Christ ever since.

I gave my life back to Christ, and I've been living in Christ ever since.

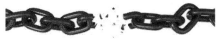

I was well on the road to raising my son to be the best man I knew he could be, but he needed to meet his grandpa. By the time my son was 10 years old, he requested to meet my dad. I prayed and prayed before calling him because it had been 10 years since our last conversation. If this was going to happen, I was going to need God to be with me. I had to keep telling myself, "I am doing this for my son. It's no longer about me." I also wanted to make sure my son was not disappointed by my father, because he was not like his other grandpa. I suspected that if he did not know how to be a good father, then he definitely didn't know how to be a good grandpa. Despite my reservations, I was willing to give it a try.

I've learned that I needed our 10-year separation, because I still had a lot of growing up to do. That space helped me to heal. It gave me more time with my heavenly Father so He could get me ready for the next journey that I was about to encounter. It's been two years now since my dad has been in mine and my son's life. Although we're navigating the relationship, it's still tough. He'll end the conversation with, "Love you and tell Tae I love him, too." I just wish he'd hold a conversation with him and try to get to know him. I had to learn to manage my expectations when dealing with my father. After looking back over my life, I realized that my healing journey started with my son. I had my child out of wedlock and went through hell throughout his baby years. It definitely took a village to raise my child. He was still my little miracle baby. In the beginning, I did not look at it that way because it was so *bad*. He was the seed I planted to grow a better relationship with my dad.

Back then, one would call me a Christian who fell and got back up again. It may have taken a while for me to find my way, but I made my way back to God. That's all that matters. I was truly a new creation. Through all the obstacles and tragedies I endured, God was still with me, walking right beside me. When times were too hard, He carried me. He was whispering in my ear, trying to get me back on the narrow path. It is obvious that God had His hands on me at a young age. He knew my earthly father wouldn't be there, but He also knew soon I would figure out that I had a heavenly Father who was with me the whole time.

God can and will deliver you from all your troubles. He says in Psalm 34:17 (King James Version), *"The righteous cry, and the Lord heareth, and delivereth them out of all their troubles."* You may have also endured a lot in your lifetime, but remember that there is always a way of escape. The enemy does not have to hold you in bondage. If you are a child of God, you need to retake your place on the throne. If you're struggling as a child of God, renounce the devil and jump on board the Jesus boat! There's healing in it.

Finally Ready to Fly

"You are responsible for your life. You can't keep blaming somebody else for your dysfunction. Life is really about moving on."

Oprah Winfrey

It took a whole lot of praying to let go of the anger and the rage. A whole lot of praying for me to no longer feel neglected and abandoned. As I grew up, I asked God plenty of times, "Why am I so angry?" He opened my eyes to a lot of things that happened to me in my life, but it all started with being fatherless. While I felt unwanted by my earthly father, my heavenly Father still chose me.

While on my journey, one of my cousins told me that if I wanted my dad in my life, I was going to have to put up with him. It took me years to understand what that really meant. It wasn't that my dad was always right; I was just adding fuel to the fire. As I learned who my father really was, I realized that she was definitely right. Some things about him might change, while others wouldn't. I had to learn to embrace the differences. Because I still love my dad, and always will, I chose to tolerate him. At the same time, I chose to pray for him. Through my

prayers, God is changing things. Over the years, I put my pride aside. I learned how to have a conversation with my dad without having an argument. I also

It wasn't that my dad was always right; I was just adding fuel to the fire.

learned that if things started to turn south, I could redirect the conversation so that my father and I wouldn't hang up the phone mad at each other. In the past, it was hard to deal with him, but I've matured and I know that God is always by my side, helping me through the relationship. I realized that you have to *want* to change. It's time to stop pointing the finger. Getting over a mountain isn't easy, but if you put in the work, and if you bring God along for the ride, He'll make it as smooth as possible. Throughout this journey, I learned to forgive my earthly father and to let go of all the anger. I also learned to embrace the joy and freedom of letting go. I knew a part of me was growing on the inside, and I loved every minute of it. I knew if I could overcome all this (and this feeling of joy was my reward), then I could overcome anything with God walking by my side.

Slowly, I have been healing over the years. I am finally free. I am walking in faith. God has ordered all of my steps. So, all I have to do is follow Him. My advice for all fathers is to embrace your children. A father is the first man a daughter will ever love. Daughters need to feel and be told they're loved, too. For anyone that's fatherless, just know that if you don't get this from your earthly father, your heavenly Father is always there to pick up the pieces.

I no longer have to be afraid of talking to my dad. I no longer have to worry about how he would react to anything I say or do. I can hold a conversation now without anger and resentment. While he is my earthly father, and I respect him and honor him, I answer to the Most High. He is my real father, and has been all my life. He has been collecting my tears and putting all my pieces back together. It's finally now time for healing and moving forward in my life. I also help others who are faced with the same problem so that, together, we can fly to our destiny.

"If you can't fly, then run; if you can't run, then walk; if you can't walk, then crawl, but whatever you do, you have to keep moving forward."

Dr. Martin Luther King, Jr.

For more information about Daunita and her fearless way of life, visit www.DaunitaSaunders.com.

SELF-REFLECTION QUESTIONS

1. How does your story relate to this one?

_____

_____

_____

_____

_____

_____

_____

2. How did being fatherless affect your childhood?

_____

_____

_____

_____

_____

_____

_____

SELF-REFLECTION QUESTIONS

3. What was most difficult about being around your friends who had both parents in the household?

_____

_____

_____

_____

_____

_____

_____

_____

4. Have you set boundaries in your relationships? If not, why?

_____

_____

_____

_____

_____

_____

_____

Fathered,
but Fatherless

Melissa Owens

"For God has not given us a spirit of fear, but of power and of love and of a sound mind."

2 Timothy 1:7, New Kings James Version

When one hears the term "fatherless," it usually refers to a person living without a father in the home. Well, I'm here to debunk the myth. My dad was in my life, but the lack of emotional support

I'm here to debunk the myth.

was challenging growing up. He was my biggest fan, but he was also the person who caused me the most hurt. I was born in 1966. In those days, married couples stayed together and families typically didn't air their *dirty laundry*. They kept their lives private and worked through their difficulties behind closed doors. Many unfortunately simply swept their issues under an imaginary rug. Men could do what they wanted and women were supposed to take it. My mother was an exception to that rule. She refused to accept infidelity, mental abuse, verbal abuse or drug abuse, so sadly, she and my dad divorced, much to his dismay.

By the time I was three years old, my mother and I were on our own. We lived with my maternal grandparents and my uncle. My grandparents had a loving, strong marriage. My grandma, who I called Nanny, was a Pentecostal, Church of God, believer. My Papaw was a devoted Catholic. My mother and her brother went to Catholic schools and attended mass weekly. My Papaw was the consistent, stable male role in my life until his death in 1986.

My dad, who has deep roots in the mountains of Appalachia, was born in Jackson County, Kentucky. His mother, my other Nanny, has rich heritage and was raised in the church. While many ministers were birthed from her family, many of her family members struggle with addiction. Satan attacks families generationally, and mine was no different. In the church, some of my fondest memories include me going with both of my grandmothers, as well as my mother. My other Papaw was hard-working and quiet. He offered words of encouragement and support on the holidays.

My dad fought hard to slay the giant called *addiction*. As a little girl, although my parents were divorced, my dad remained in my life. We saw each other often. He picked me up for school every morning and took me out for breakfast. We listened to R. W. Schambach on the radio so I could understand who God was. He tried to cover me with a blanket of right despite doing so much wrong. He knew the truth and wanted the best for me, but he didn't choose the best path for himself. A gripping stronghold of mental illness, accompanied by drug usage, kept him bound. Addiction is real.

In those days, I looked up to my father. I didn't see the error of his ways or the demons he faced. He was *my dad*. He told me I was the prettiest, the smartest, the best. He told me I could accomplish anything. I believed him. He promised never to lie to me and, to my knowledge, he never did. He was my dad and I was his little girl. We were in this together.

As I matured, things changed. I noticed he started having more and more mood swings, but he still wanted to see me all the time. I wasn't sure all our visits were always about me. Could my dad have ulterior motives? Could I be the link to staying connected to my mother? Lots of things swirled in my head, but nothing could prepare me for what I would find out next.

My father was good at hiding his sickness from me. Everything he took was prescribed by a physician, so that made it *medicine*. He didn't smoke marijuana, drink alcohol or smoke cigarettes. His drugs of choice came from prescribing physicians. He took uppers and downers. When he was on amphetamines, he could stay awake for days. When on opiates or barbiturates, he slept for days. I never knew who was coming to pick me up for weekend visits, taking me to elementary school, or driving me to any other activities because of his inconsistency. I was afraid, embarrassed, confused and worried that my future would mirror my dad's addiction. I often wondered, *"If his blood flows through my veins, will I be like him?"*

"Missy, don't do as I do. Do as I say," he often told me. I wasn't sure if his behavior was due to the drug abuse, or if this was *really* him. My father was very controlling. He tried

Don't do as I do. Do as I say.

to control my friendships and my relationships. I was embarrassed and often feared how he would behave around others. Would he be wasted, angry, aggressive and bullying, or would he be godly and spiritual?

When I was in the sixth grade, I wanted to be a cheerleader. The coach and older team members told me that I was a 'shoe-in' to make the squad. I was nervous and struggled with my own self-confidence. But, when my father heard that I was trying out, he called our home and put a stop to it immediately. He threatened me and my mother, "If I catch her down there cheering, I will come down there, snatch her off the field, and beat her hind end!"

On the day of my high school graduation, I was so excited. We were preparing to leave, when the phone rang. It was my father. He wasn't calling to tell me how proud he was of me or to tell me that he would meet us at the auditorium. He was calling to say that he wasn't coming. He said graduating from high school wasn't a big deal.

"Anybody can do that," he said.

I argued back at first. I was the first person on both sides of our immediate family to ever graduate high school. Then, I burst into tears. It was a rollercoaster ride that I learned to navigate with fear. He preyed on those who couldn't fight back, and I was one of them. There are many things I would have loved to have participated in, but because of my father's controlling nature I was too afraid. When his aggressive side reared its ugly head, he often lost his temper and become violent and abusive. Fear kept winning, and my heart kept breaking. Sometimes in life, not being there at all is far better than being there and breaking hearts consistently.

I introduced my father to my fiancé in 1991 and they connected well. I started planning my wedding a few months later, thinking my dad would show up to give me away, like most fathers do at their daughter's wedding. My mother ended up giving me away. I know that wasn't traditional but, up to this point in my life, there wasn't a whole lot that had been *traditional*. The first six years of my twelve-year marriage were wonderful. We were happy and in love. My husband knew Jesus Christ and committed his life to Him. Life was good, until one day my husband had to have knee surgery.

The old high school sports injuries resurfaced after many years. This brought about a downhill spiral, which triggered that old familiar spirit that he knew from his youth. He started using narcotics for pain, which ultimately led to an ever-growing need for them. He, too, had been prescribed them initially by a physician. No wonder my father and my husband got along so well. My husband and my father had something in common. They were both addicts. Both men, who vowed to love me, chose narcotics over me. The

Both men, who vowed to love me, chose narcotics over me.

internal processing and rejection felt overwhelming. I kept it inside mostly, until I exploded into fits of anger, rage and tears, followed by depression. I tried to make my marriage work. I was holding on to something dead. I remained married another six years until the marriage finally ended mutually in a divorce.

I was afraid, angry, hurt and bitter. But I knew that the God I served would help me and deliver me if I would praise my way through my circumstances. I wanted to run away, but I had two children to think about. I was in rebellion mode and thinking selfishly. I wanted to hurt him the way I'd been hurt all those years. The infamous mistress known as the *pill bottle* stole my dad's heart many years before, and now she had taken dominion over my husband's, too. I said and did things I am not proud of. I resented drugs and addicts. I hated addiction and I felt victimized, even though I never took a pill.

Relinquishing Control

"I prayed to the Lord, and he answered me. He freed me from all my fears."

Psalm 34:4, New Living Translation

Although I felt victimized in many ways, I refused to live as a victim. I learned through the years to control my emotions and keep going. I had to deal with the cards I was dealt. The life I fanaticized about with wealth and grandeur was just a dream. I was a woman going through divorce, raising two children, and facing an extreme lifestyle change. As I took one step forward, depression crept in, causing me to take two steps back. My emotions fluctuated. I loved. I hated. I felt free and ready to move on to the next chapter one moment, then frightened and so uncertain of how I would rear my children alone, pay my bills, and take care of my home without my husband the next. I thought, *"Even if he is messed up, he is still there."* I wondered how I could do this all alone.

I was trying to find who I was. I was trying to find me again. I had lost myself. I felt I needed to lose weight, cut my hair, change the outward so the inside could feel better. I wanted to take control of the things I could, since the things I had no control of were spinning out of control—and fast. I felt like I was in the middle of a whirlwind. My life was flying by me and I had to grab it as it passed. It still passed. Life moves on, and you must move with it. I had to go to work, take care of my children, face my critics and keep living. I did it. I survived divorce.

The old adage says that time heals all wounds. It does, but so does prayer and talking to family and friends. I poured my thoughts and feelings out in some of the strangest ways. Being a Pentecostal girl, my strength came from being surrounded by prayer. I had to release all the anger, resentment and

I acknowledged my healing when I relinquished control and submitted my will to God's will.

betrayal, and allow the comfort of the Holy Spirit to mend me. Little by little, I improved and I could see light shining through the darkness. I learned to forgive my husband for his poor choices as I healed inwardly. I realized my husband, like my father, didn't hurt me personally; they were both men who had illnesses. I acknowledged my healing when I relinquished control and submitted my will to God's will. I learned that we must endure our process. My inner strength came from my established relationship with Jesus Christ.

I remained single for three years, raising my children with the help of my mother. She retired early to help me with my special needs son and my daughter so I could continue to work. It wasn't easy, but I had to get my identity back. That meant being single for a while. I needed to heal from the devastation. We make our own choices in life. He made his, as my father did, and I made mine. I took control of my life and stopped exposing myself to the things that caused me pain. I wasn't the forgotten daughter or the broken wife. I was now the single mother. When Jesus is all you have, you find He is all you need.

God of the Details

"There is no fear in love; but perfect love casts out fear, because fear involves torment. But he who fears has not been made perfect in love."

1 John 4:18, New King James Version

Later, I met Bishop Patrick D. Owens. His ex-spouse also had addiction problems and mental health issues. He was raising his children alone, and so was I. It didn't hurt that he met all my criteria for my next husband. He was 6'4", dark and handsome. He was a man of great wisdom, character and integrity. He was worthy of all my respect. Patrick was rearing three biological children, two sons and a daughter, and a niece who belonged to his ex-wife's sister. We met for the first time on his birthday. He was shy and he barely made eye contact. I wondered how this man, who was so articulate behind the computer screen, could be the same person. I was confused. I questioned whether I would ever go back out with him again.

I asked God, "Surely, he couldn't be the one? He won't even look at me!"

I even went into the restroom to call another boyfriend to bail me out, if necessary, and had him on standby. God truly has a sense of humor. Somehow, Patrick must have known something was up, or the Holy Spirit did some major work on him from the time I made the call until the time I came out. He gained confidence and his personality shined brightly.

On June 19, 2009, we formed our *Brady Bunch* with three boys and three girls. God is good! Blending a family comes with its share of difficulties, but we did it. Eight people successfully made it in a three-bedroom house. There were visits to psychologists and doctors, many therapy sessions and hours of prayer. How could we fail with the Lord by our side? The one thing I know is that in every situation, in moments of weakness, as a divorced, single mother praying for my blended family and feeling helpless and hopeless, our heavenly Father will never leave us nor forsake us. He will carry us through until the end. He is forever constant.

I know this same Jesus, who watched over me as a child, carried me through my youth, sustained me through my poor choices, and shadowed me in the darkness of divorce, will also carry others through their most painful times in life. I am the daughter of an addict, the ex-wife of an addict, and the mother of a son born with special needs.

Labels do not define me.

But those labels do not define me. I am so much more than that. I am an overcomer. Fear tried to stunt my growth, but today I am *fearless*.

After serving for twenty-eight years in ministry, God moved Bishop Owens and I into full-time pastoral roles in Eaton, Ohio. We became the pastors of Eaton Church of God, which later became Grace and Fire Worship Center under our leadership. I had never been a First Lady or a right hand to my husband in ministry, but God was preparing me for something greater. We remained in Eaton as lead pastors approximately seven years. While serving there, the Filling Station Women's Ministry was born.

In 2012, I had no idea that God wanted me to lead women, but I trusted Him completely. I had never led a ministry before, but I heard the voice of the Lord say, "Get out of the boat." I initially started the Filling Station to encourage and inform women locally, but I found that women drove from surrounding areas to be refilled, refreshed, refueled and empowered. They wanted *something real*. God called me to be a catalyst to catapult others. He called me to provide a place of healing, safety, transparency and comfort for women to drink from the well that never runs dry.

A year ago, God relocated our ministry into a new season. We currently pastor at Fairfield Church of God in Fairfield, Ohio. The Filling Station Women's Ministry is open to all women. My vision is for all women from all walks of life to find whatever they need in His presence. If one needs salvation, healing, deliverance, breakthrough, encouragement, an *oil change* or a *tire rotation*, they can come to the Filling Station and meet the Great Physician, the Master Mechanic, and taste and see that the Lord is good. Their needs are met as they press into His presence through praise, worship and prayer. The Holy Spirit never disappoints. Those who seek Him will find Him when they search for Him with their whole hearts. I am so thankful, grateful and humbled that when I searched for Him, I found Him. He is the one who caused a child from a broken home, in an era when parents were supposed to stay together, to rise above the stigma of labels to become fearless. He makes me brave.

My confidence grew as I matured as a believer in Jesus Christ. After accepting Him as my personal Lord and Savior, I was no longer defined by man's definition. I started to believe in who God said I was and could be. I am a Christian woman who, despite my best efforts, ended up divorced in my first marriage. My children grew up for many years without a father in the home. Today,

When we give others permission to make decisions we should make for ourselves, we lose our power.

their biological dad is clean, sober and in their lives. I prayed for that. To God be all the glory. I am a woman who has made mistakes, poor choices and bad decisions. Still, His grace is sufficient. I have failed many times, but I am so thankful to know that even when I failed Him, He never gave up on me. He was always hovering, calling, protecting, covering and keeping me safe.

You, too, can persevere. You can make it! You are fearfully and wonderfully made. Your identity is not based on anyone or anything other than you and your Creator. Your validation comes from above. *"He whom the Son sets free is free indeed."* When we give others permission to make decisions we should make for ourselves, we lose our power. Allowing others to control us will weaken us. I am now walking in freedom and trusting in the One who orders my steps. We must allow Him to fill us up with what He has for us. If we are full of fear, pain, insecurity and rejection, we will not have room to be filled with His love, joy, peace, healing, wholeness and forgiveness. Empty yourself first by casting your cares on Jesus. Ask Him to help you through prayer. He is listening.

Father, I pray for anyone reading this book. I pray for inner healing. I pray for peace in the release. Freedom is found when we let go of fear. I bind the generational stronghold of addiction over lives today. I pray for the addict and the victim, and I release forgiveness and love, in Jesus' name. I pray for joy to be restored. God is love. Allow the God of all love to bring comfort to your wounded soul, to your wounded spirit, in Jesus' name. He has truly brought me *From Fatherless to Fearless* through faith and trusting in the God who cannot and will not fail.

For more information about Melissa and her fearless way of life, visit www.MelissaOwensMinistries.com.

SELF-REFLECTION QUESTIONS

1. Have you ever had someone tell you one thing, but show you something different? If yes, how did you feel?

   _____

   _____

   _____

   _____

   _____

   _____

2. To be controlled by fear is paralyzing and debilitating. It will stunt your growth. Can you describe a time on your journey to fearlessness that you defeated the giant called fear?

   _____

   _____

   _____

   _____

   _____

   _____

SELF-REFLECTION QUESTIONS

3. God cares about the *little things*. On your pursuit to wholeness, share some details with God. Write down the desires of your heart.

_____

_____

_____

_____

_____

_____

4. Faith triumphs over fear every time. Describe a time when you allowed your faith to propel you forward.

_____

_____

_____

_____

_____

_____

_____

_____

Aborted Abortion

LaTerra Wise

"Many are the plans in a person's heart, but it is the
Lord's purpose that prevails."

Proverbs 19:21, New International Version

Before I had a body, I had purpose. And from the time I was conceived, the enemy has tried to kill it. What does that have to do with being fatherless? Everything! My life as a fatherless daughter has been a struggle to find love and acceptance, while also trying to find myself. The search for a father's love exposed me to experience after experience that tried to break my spirit and keep me from fulfilling my God-given purpose. It all started with one decision by my parents before I was even born.

Children were never part of my father's original plans. So, imagine what went through his mind as a 19-year-old young man when he found out his 17-year-old girlfriend was pregnant with their first child. He hadn't figured out his *own* life, so being responsible for someone else's was completely out of the question. His solution was for my mother to have an abortion. After some  discussion, she agreed. It seemed as if the *My life was about to end before* enemy had won. My life was about to end *it had even begun.* before it had even begun, but God had a  different plan. When my mother went to have the abortion, she found out she was too far into the pregnancy to have the procedure. Faced with the reality of parenthood, my father chose to walk away. The truth of my beginning wasn't revealed to me until years after the damage of fatherlessness had already settled deep down into my soul.

My early childhood relationship with my father can best be described as forced. His parents adored me, so they encouraged him to be a part of my life, but to no avail. While I did see him periodically at Christmastime and on summer break, there was a lack of consistency. We didn't have a bond, and looking back,

I can't remember him saying, "I love you" or receiving any type of affection from him. As an adult, I can see how that's shaped my hesitant reaction to receiving affection from my own children. It is one of the many difficult lessons I've had to unlearn over time.

Although I didn't know it at the time, my father had internal demons he battled with daily, which kept him at a distance. The only thing I knew was that my father wasn't there for me like my friends' fathers, and my adolescent mind desperately tried to figure out why. I internalized his absence and wondered what it was about me that was unlovable. Why wasn't I worth knowing? I didn't realize that if the enemy couldn't kill me physically through abortion, he would try to kill me emotionally by using my father's absence.

I wasn't one of those kids who could say my father was my hero. On a bad day, I referred to him as my donor. On a good day, he was a familiar stranger that I hated because, although he was a part of me, he was not an active presence in my life. The seeds of self-doubt, low self-esteem, unworthiness and inadequacy were planted in me by the broken relationship with my father. I never fit in with my family or my peers because they were loud and expressive, while I was the quiet introvert. Because my father wasn't around, I didn't know that my timid nature came from him. As a result, I questioned whether I was enough and I lived my life from that place of uncertainty. I silenced my voice and let other people define my worth.

From the time I was five years old, I found my worth in sexuality. Several cousins and classmates acted as if my body was their playground. I didn't have my father around to teach me differently, so I let their idea of me become my identity. I placed my value in my body, and my clothes became shorter and tighter as I got older. Because of the broken relationship with my father, as a teen, I travelled down a path of self-destruction. From the outside looking in, I was a happy person. I had friends. I went to football games and dances. I even excelled academically. But at the age of 13, I became depressed and contemplated suicide.

On the night I decided I was going take my life, God gave me a glimpse of the purpose the enemy was trying to kill. He showed me that my story and all the pain I had survived would be used to impact the lives of others. I didn't fully know how that would manifest, but I knew enough to trust that God fulfills His promises. I was raised in church and went faithfully with my grandmother and mother. But it wasn't until my first encounter with God that I gained the perspective that my pain had greater

God revealed that suicide was not the answer.

meaning. After God revealed that suicide was not the answer, I went to a service where a friend of mine came to me and cried on my shoulder. I could feel the weight of the pain she carried, and God gave me the words to comfort her. Up until then, I thought I was alone in my pain. In that moment, I realized I wasn't alone and that I could be a vessel for God to bring healing to others. I was finally starting to learn myself, but there were still missing pieces.

I would love to say shortly after I had that revelation, my relationship with my father was magically repaired and all my problems went away, but that's so far from the truth. At that time, it was non-existent. My father lived less than five minutes away from me, and I never knew until I moved to the other side of town. My stepfather came home one day and told me that my dad was in his car because he was giving him a ride. He never came in to see me, and I wasn't interested in going outside to see him. By then, the damage had been done. I was content knowing I was a fatherless daughter. I let that become my identity and my crutch. It hurt, but I was in denial, even when I thought I had let it go. I believed I didn't need my father. I didn't realize that, without knowing him, I couldn't fully know myself. From that point on, there was a void in my soul that I desperately tried to fill.

For a while, I lived a double life. By the age of 16, most people knew me as a *church girl*. I was active in the youth ministry. I was a youth usher and a praise dancer, but I was still broken. I reached a point where I just wanted to be numb. If I could feel, I knew I'd feel the pain. I didn't want to feel the pain. Consequently, sex, alcohol and marijuana became my coping mechanisms. I often drank until I blacked out and bad decisions quickly followed. I stopped going to church because I refused to be a hypocrite. I spiraled out of control, and for three years I lost my mind. The self-destructive course I was on led to me being raped by someone I called a friend. While the trauma of that experience would change most people, I fell right back into the same behaviors as before. When faced with choices, my fatherlessness made decisions on my behalf. When speaking, my fatherlessness spoke for me. It

When speaking, my fatherlessness spoke for me.

justified the mess that my life had become. I was satisfied with being broken. That was all I would ever be…until I met a man who changed my life. Our relationship opened the door for me to find myself and claim my healing.

Finding Me by Loving Him

"A strong marriage requires loving your spouse even in those moments when they aren't being lovable; it means believing in them even when they struggle to believe in themselves."

Dave Willis

I met this charismatic, funny, handsome man who challenged me in August of 2002. By December of the same year, I was pregnant with our first child. I took two tests just to be sure it was real before I shared the news with him. I was nervous. The first words out of my mouth after I showed him those two pink lines were, "You don't have to stay. I'll be fine on my own." He looked at me like I was crazy and quickly calmed my fears by reassuring me that, no matter what decision I made, he would be there. He let me know that he loved me and that this journey was one we would take together. I was overwhelmed by his commitment to me and our future. I instantly knew this man was different from anyone I had encountered before. I could trust him with my whole heart.

Our daughter was born in September of 2003 and the bond she has with her father was instant. He showered her with affection. He was everything I wanted *my* father to be. My fatherless issues crept in and I found myself envying their relationship. I suppressed those feelings for as long as I could.

But when I could no longer ignore them, I knew it was time to change. That amazing man became my husband in 2008. By then, we had two children. To the outsiders looking in, we had it all together. But I was still operating from that place of brokenness. I thought my issues would go away by me being a good wife and mother, but that wasn't the case. I still didn't know who I was as a woman. So, when my husband didn't validate me, I searched for it elsewhere. My fatherless issues almost led to the end of our marriage after I had an affair. Cheating was a familiar behavior, which I used to guard my heart from being hurt. I never cared about the other person's feelings--until I saw the pain in my husband's eyes. He forgave me, and I made a conscious decision to never see that look on his face again.

The love of my husband and our children is truly a reflection of God's love for me. That love broke down the walls I had built up. That love restored my faith. I needed to do the deep work within, and my husband was not afraid to help me through it. My husband played an integral part in my healing. He saw the weight I carried from being a fatherless daughter, but he still stayed. I showed him my scars, and he covered and protected me. He showed me a father's love as he cared for our children. He showed me true unconditional love. I returned to church and rededicated my life to God. Every Sunday, the pastor preached the Word and it chipped away at my walls. God met me at the altar every week as I cried out for healing and restoration. I made a faith exchange. I gave God my broken pieces, and in return, I received joy, peace and love. I wanted to be everything God intended for me to be.

My grandmother took on the role of babysitter for my children after school, and eventually, my father came around more. My kids loved him. He was an awesome Pop-Pop, but I was

I chose healing.

still hesitant to let him in. As he became more consistent in my children's lives, I had to make a choice: Do I want to hold on to my anger and pain, or do I want to be healed? I chose healing. If I wanted something different for myself, I had to do something different.

Two conversations confirmed my decision. The first was with my mother. When I was pregnant with my twins, she finally told me that my father never wanted children. At that time, however, she left out the part about the abortion. The second conversation, which was with my grandmother, finally gave the first one meaning. My grandmother revealed to me that my father never had a relationship with his dad. In fact, he was denied by his father's entire side of the family.

As I heard more of the details, I better understood that my father couldn't give me the love I needed because it wasn't given to him. I'm not exactly sure when it happened, and I can't really say how it happened, but God restored my relationship with my father. I released him of my expectations of how his love should look. I made a conscious effort to meet him where he was and accept the love he could give. When I forgave my father for all the pain his absence caused, I freed myself from the idea that I wasn't good enough. There was nothing I was lacking that would have made him stay. When I let go of the expectations that I had for *him*, I found *myself*.

You see, that void I tried to fill for so long was not created because I lacked relationship with my father; it was created because I lacked relationship with *myself*. All the time I spent hating my father subconsciously caused me to hate myself. I was so much like my father. I shared his creative spirit, his calm demeanor and his stubborn nature. My face is a perfect blend of both my parents, so I learned to love the features that reminded me of him. By letting go of the hate, hurt and anger, I learned to fully love and accept who I was. I embraced my quiet nature and my creative spirit. I accepted the fact that my father's absence did not deny or delay God's purpose for my life. That realization allowed me to step into the purpose God called me to fulfill.

You Can't Abort Purpose

"Before I formed you in the womb I knew you, before you were born I set you apart; I appointed you as a prophet to the nations."

Jeremiah 1:5, New International Version

Stepping into God's plan for my life meant reconnecting with one of my first loves: writing. It was my passion at a young age, especially writing poetry. Poetry was always a part of me, and it was one of the greatest tools for healing in my life. Writing poetry allowed me to channel the pain of my past experiences into something beautiful that connected with other women. It allowed me to take control of my narrative. I shared my truth, my pain and my healing. My first book, *Design of a Woman: Heart, Mind, Body & Soul*, was the fulfillment of the vision God gave me as a suicidal teenager. It was the beginning of a journey to work in my calling by helping others heal. The road wasn't easy; I questioned whether I was worthy or capable of leading others on their healing journeys. Every time I had those thoughts, I met a woman

This was the work I was born to do.

or young girl I was able to encourage and comfort through my story. God confirmed His words to me and assured me that this was the work I was born to do.

In 2016, I founded 'Woman Unmasked' with the mission of helping women see the purpose beyond their pain and the beauty beyond their masks. The first event I co-hosted was a seminar called 'From Brokenness to Breakthrough'. One of the speakers was my mother, who was also one of the co-authors of my book. During her speech, she told her truth. I sat on the side listening intently as she told the story of her first pregnancy, which was her pregnancy with me. Right there in the room, along with 25 other women, I found out I was supposed to be aborted. I sat in shock, not able to process what I had just heard. And I was supposed to speak next. When she introduced me to the audience, she said something that was a game changer for my life. As she closed her speech, she reminded them, "You can't abort purpose, and this is that child."

When the event was over, after everything had been cleaned up and I was home alone in my bedroom, I cried and thanked God for my life. I realized that the purpose God had for me was bigger than me. It made me realize that everything I had been through—fatherlessness, molestation, depression and rape—was meant to kill me before I could know the whole truth. That revelation lit a fire inside me. I thought about every time I questioned if I was really doing what God called me to do, and every time I started and stopped because I was afraid of what people would think. What God put inside of me is so powerful that the enemy tried everything in his power to destroy it. Yet, I'm still standing. I had survived his every attack. I committed right then and there in my bedroom, that no matter what, I wouldn't give up. I *couldn't* give up. I committed to living my life fully. How dare I do anything less! How dare I accept anything but the will of God for my life! In that moment, I owned my truth—the good, the bad, the ugly.

No longer would I be ashamed of my past because it all had purpose. It was a training ground for everything God has called me to be and do. I lost guilt, shame and fear, and I found my voice. I started sharing my story to help others heal, and I created a space for other women to do the same. The 'Woman Unmasked' podcast is where women share their stories of overcoming, and they provide tips and tools to help others do the same. One guest said this is not just a podcast, but a movement. I have truly embraced that vision. This is a movement—a chain reaction of healing that God has allowed me to facilitate.

I fearlessly and unapologetically walk in the truth of the woman I am.

I fearlessly and unapologetically walk in the truth of the woman I am. Because of God, I am fearfully and wonderfully made (Psalm 139:14, English Standard Version). I have a divine assignment to complete. Being fatherless is not the totality of who I am. I am a mother, wife, life coach, speaker, host and author, all of which was birthed from God, using the very broken pieces of fatherlessness. The reality of my life is that my father didn't want me. Although it is a hard pill to swallow, I realize that God wanted and needed me for His purpose.

I love my father and I know he loves me. I can say that now and truly mean it. Loving him doesn't mean our relationship is perfect. It simply means I accept my father just as he is. It also means that I don't allow myself to be defined by the moments of his absence. I understand the ebb and flow of our relationship, and that has made all the difference in our lives.

***

To the woman whose heart was broken by her father, know that you are loved. I know you may be searching for your father's love in every man you meet, but trust me, you are *enough*. Just as you are, you are worthy. Your heart is worthy of healing. Your mind is worthy of peace. Your life is worthy of joy. For whatever reason, your father wasn't able to stay. It's okay because God was there, and He'll always remain by your side. Just as God had a plan for my life and a purpose beyond my fatherlessness, He has a plan for you. His plan for your life is greater than any one piece of you. Fatherless is not who you are. Damaged is not who you are. Don't allow yourself to be defined by the brokenness within you. There is a work for you to complete, and every pain born out of your fatherlessness is preparation for that work. It's time to stop defining yourself by the one who didn't want you and embrace who you are by the One who needs you. Let go of the hurt, guilt, shame and anger.

Understand that when you release yourself from your fatherless issues, and choose to take the path of forgiveness, God will reveal the truth of who you are. He calls you wonderful. He calls you strong. He calls you more than a conqueror. That is the truth of who you are. Hold on to that truth, so when the enemy tries to bring contrary thoughts to your mind, you can fight back.

You don't need validation from your father or any other man; you won't find it there. Your validation comes from embracing all of who you are. In case you are like me and you never heard it from your father, "I love you." You are special and there is so much more in store for you!

For more information about LaTerra and her fearless way of life, visit www.LaTerraWise.com.

SELF-REFLECTION QUESTIONS

1. What purpose has being fatherless equipped you to fulfill?

   _____

   _____

   _____

   _____

   _____

   _____

2. What dysfunctional beliefs are you holding onto as a result of being

   fatherless? How can you release those beliefs?

   _____

   _____

   _____

   _____

   _____

   _____

SELF-REFLECTION QUESTIONS

3. What has fatherlessness protected you from?

_____

_____

_____

_____

_____

_____

_____

4. How can you use the lessons you learned through your fatherlessness?

_____

_____

_____

_____

_____

_____

Chapter 6

Destined Beyond Divorce

Genoa Peak

"The eyes of the Lord are in every place,
beholding the evil and the good."

Proverbs 15:3, King James Version

My earliest childhood memory was waking up to the sun shining brightly through my bedroom window and hearing a beautiful duet of my parents singing to each other while preparing breakfast. It gave me such a sense of well-being. You could feel the love in our home. My father's mother had passed away, so my father and my aunt Helen (his eldest sister) decided to take in their younger siblings. I loved having my aunt and uncle with us. We were a close-knit family, so we spent a lot of time together. There were plenty of family outings, and my father was big on education. As a three-year-old, my father patiently taught me how to tie my shoes while sitting on the living room floor. On outings to Woodslake, I would ride on his shoulders while playing in the water. Because my father worked a lot, the times we spent as a family were precious. Me and my sisters would ride in the car with my mom to my father's job to pick up his paycheck. They would talk for a few minutes, he'd kiss her, and then he'd reach into the car to ruffle our heads affectionately before he went back into work.

One day, I was awakened out of my sleep by my mother and father shouting at each other. She yelled at me and my sisters to get in the car. They began tussling while she was trying to leave because my father wanted her to stay.

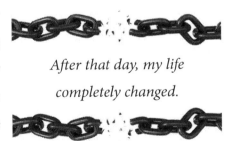

After that day, my life completely changed.

My last memory of that day is of us in the car speeding down the street while my father tried to chase us. After that day, my life completely changed. We arrived at my grandparents' house. There were other family members living there, so we had to squeeze in. It was me, my two little sisters and my mom. There was no more father, aunt or uncle—not to mention, no more space of my own. Soon enough, I would find out that this also meant *no more childhood.*

I instantly had more responsibility than I'd ever had. At five years old, I was the oldest. My mom expected me to step up to the plate and learn to take care of my sisters, something I never had to do before. I saw my father on and off, but it was never the same. His last words are still deeply embedded in my mind and spirit: "Take care of your mother and look out for your sisters. Be a good example for them." On that day, he passed the tainted baton to me for a race I couldn't run. His words pierced my heart, but they would be the map for how I lived my life many years to come. My parents ended up getting a divorce, and all I got was the short end of the stick.

We only lived with my grandparents for a little while before moving into our own place. There was always a lot of people over our house. They never brought anything over, except themselves. There was company there when we woke up in the morning and when we went to bed at night. They were moochers, always eating our food and taking things meant for me and my sisters. We moved a lot, so I was always the new kid at school.

In one fell swoop, it was like my childhood disappeared. I ceased to matter, except for the work I was supposed to do. No one looked out for me, although there was family around. Mom's philosophy was, "What goes on in this house, stays in this house." I tested this to my own detriment. I was only rewarded based on what I was told to do. All chores had to be done before bedtime; otherwise, me and my sisters would be picked up from school the next day just to get in trouble. My mother, as a newly divorced woman with three young daughters, became a target for all kinds of unsavory people with evil plans toward her children. They acted like they cared about us around our mother but, behind closed doors, it was different. Some tried to kiss me and my sisters in the mouth while others felt us up while hugging us. We were surrounded by pedophiles in disguise as friends, play aunts, play uncles and the like.

To drown out her pain, my mother became a party girl, and my sisters and I became victims of her lifestyle. We were molested, mistreated and abused without the watchful eye of a loving father. We were the victims of a hurting parent, who was trying to fill the void in her life with partying and alcohol. Although my mother worked, she still frequently went to clubs. One time, some older boys were babysitting us and decided they wanted to play house. I was only six or seven years old when the oldest one said I was his wife. He took me in the room and molested me. On another occasion, my mother's friend's daughter molested me during a sleepover. In addition, I had an uncle that had married into the family

I was happy when my mother left us at home alone. At least no one could molest me.

that let me stay up to watch TV after sending the younger children to bed. He also tried to make advances, and even offered me money. Things of this nature went on quite a bit. I was happy when my mother left us at home alone. At least no one could molest me.

Because we moved around, I went to eleven schools before I finally graduated. My mother's drinking escalated to the point that life was unbearable. I was accused of all manner of things and called foul names. I was beaten for something someone else said I was doing. I was so angry that I even ran away from home, only to find the world was even more dangerous.

With my mom and I at odds, we were sent to live with our father. My sisters and I were already so damaged by all the things that happened in our lives after the divorce that there was no way going to live with him could save us as a family. I wanted my parents to change their ways and think about how their actions affected their children. The devil was after my life, and it continued to show.

When my sisters and I went to live with our father, our mother told us it was only temporary. She began travelling with her friends. My father sat us down and had a long talk with us, but we failed to get the message. He told us to unpack and that we weren't going anywhere. But we insisted that mom was coming back for us. We settled into a routine of school, chores and hanging out with our cousins that lived around the block. However, our belongings stayed packed because we knew she'd come back and we'd have to move again. Mom would call and make promises, but she never came to get us.

By the time I was in tenth grade, I was pregnant by an older guy who was already out of school. I was looking for love and acceptance. Once my father found out, he forced me to have an abortion, making me feel ashamed, hurt and numb. My relationship with my father got even worse. Even though I knew Jesus, I still had very low self-esteem. I didn't have anyone to emotionally support me in a positive manner. I wanted more for my life, but I didn't know how to get it, so I traded sex for a semblance of love. I wanted the great love affairs that I read about in my Harlequin romance novels.

I traded sex for a semblance of love.

In the novels, no matter what happened, everything always worked out for the heroine in the stories. She always got the guy and the ring.

It wasn't long before I caught a sexually transmitted disease (STD). Many things went through my mind. I was really scared and didn't know what to do. Back then, the clinic came to the high school, spoke to the student, and took them in for treatment, without parental consent. After my treatment, things went back to normal at school—at least I thought. One day, I was at track practice when my lower abdomen started hurting. I left practice early and went home. I went to the doctor immediately. They performed emergency surgery because I was pregnant in my tube. My father didn't know about the STD that caused me to be in this condition. During recovery, the doctor who did the procedure came to see me and my father. He told me I'd probably never have children because of the damage inside. Not only did he remove one of my tubes, but he saw that my other tube was mangled as well. His words hurt me to my core. I wanted to have a family one day, but he made me believe that was it for me. It was a very scary situation, and my father and aunt did what they could to comfort me.

After all the turmoil, I still didn't stop searching for something or someone to fill the void in my heart. I knew Jesus, but my relationship with Him was lacking trust. Problems at home had gotten worse, and now I was being looked at as the child that could only do wrong. During my senior year of school, I became pregnant once again, but not without consequences. I felt this would be my only chance to become a mother. I didn't know that it would cost me what was left of my already *threadbare* relationship with my father. I felt like a ghost in the house. There was rarely any conversation, just instructions regarding the household. As the eldest, I carried the weight of my parents' hopes and dreams, and I had once again let them down. I had let *him* down – my father – and in turn, I was let down and thrown away emotionally.

It was hard drawing away from the deep hurt, but I had to think about the life I was carrying. So, I concentrated on my studies to make sure I graduated. I made plans for how I would take care of myself and my child. There was little joy for the baby. I was just an unwed teen mother headed toward a hard life.

Healing is a Process

"Lord, be gracious to us; we long for you. Be our strength every morning, our salvation in time of distress."

Isaiah 33:2, New International Version

Over the years, my father and I grew further apart. I was thankful to my uncle Myron, who started taking me with him to choir rehearsals, then church, at a young age. He set the foundation for me to know Jesus Christ.

I sang in the choir and one day, after hearing the message of salvation, I felt compelled to go up to the front and receive Jesus. I felt better than I had my entire life. I had comfort and hope for the first time ever.

I attended church every Saturday for choir rehearsal and Sunday for service. We lived across town, so I walked, singing gospel songs all the way there. I started reading the Bible and other inspirational books about salvation. I hung out with the Christian youth at church. I grew fast in some areas, while moving along slowly in others. I lived

I lived two lives: who I was at home and the "alive" me at church.

two lives: who I was at home and the "alive" me at church. I wish I could say I never broke that fellowship, but my life was tempestuous at best. Through the highs and lows of my teen years, church, my relationship with the Lord and my relationship with uncle Myron, who wouldn't let me go, no matter what was going on, are the biggest parts of why I'm here sharing with you right now.

I married and had three more children, for a total of four. It was time for me to take responsibility for my own family. I became to my children whom I wished my parents had been to me. Many people say that daughters marry their fathers or exact opposites. When I met my husband, my son was five months old. I was going into the Marines. I met him on my last night out before going to the induction center. He was handsome, fun and very attentive. I really didn't think I'd see him again, but I ended up not going into the Marines, as planned, because of a medical condition. I was very disappointed, worrying about how I was going to take care of my son. That's when our relationship began. He called me and we started dating. He loved and took care of me and my son. We married and everything started out great, but the cares of life and not enough problem-solving skills made our marriage more challenging. He turned to drugs and alcohol, and I turned to church.

As a child of divorce, I knew the pitfalls, but that wasn't enough to keep me from falling. My marriage lasted a tumultuous 15 years. Toward the last few years, it was more about maintaining my family. Things weren't going well for him. His job ended and he didn't have a high school diploma, so bills piled up. I worked, but didn't make a lot of money. We didn't have the tools to weather the storm, so the storm raged and ended in a way I knew too well: divorce. This decision started the cycle for my children.

Through the blessings of the Lord and the prayers of my grandma, I made it through this seemingly endless period. One caring person can make the difference! The Word says that every man must work out his own soul's salvation, and that is what I had to do daily! I was fighting myself. My self-esteem was low and I wanted someone, anyone, to help. I wanted to live a good life with the values that I saw at church for my children. I wanted them to have a childhood, safe from harm, so they would be all that God created them to be.

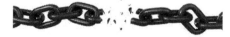

I didn't have money, so I gave them something better: their own relationship with our Creator.

As I grew in the Lord, my children grew with me. I didn't have money, so

I gave them something better: their own relationship with our Creator. Proverbs 22:6 says, *"Train up a child in the way he should go: and when he is old, he will not depart from it."* That was my mission. As I planted those seeds, I let God be the God of their lives, not me. They are adults now. I pray for them and their families, and give them godly wisdom. My mission is to break down the strongholds of my generation. Proverbs 13:22 says, *"A good man leaveth an inheritance to his children's children..."* It's important to leave something besides words. They not only need my journey, but they also should use my life as a stepping stone. I want to pass the baton to my children so they can have a better life than I did.

Nothing is Ever Wasted

"He hath made every thing beautiful in his time:..."

Ecclesiastes 3:11, King James Version

As I've studied God's Word, and walked the path daily that He has for me, I discovered that I have to be deliberate in *being* whom God created me to be. It's not always easy, but it is doable. I've used the trauma from my life to learn about grace, mercy and healing, which is what I found in Jesus Christ. I share this, not only to my own children and grandchildren, but also nieces, nephews, young cousins and friends. I've learned the true meaning of growing in grace is helping someone else to avoid life's pitfalls and sharing where that grace comes from. My pastor in Michigan always taught us

There's only God-incidences.

that experience is not the best teacher, someone else's is. Currently, I drive public transportation for a living, and I come in contact with people from all walks of life every day. It gives me the opportunity to connect and share many of life's hard-learned lessons with others. I don't believe in coincidences. There's only God-incidences. I share my story as I am led by Him. I prayerfully lead people away from disastrous decisions back to God.

My passion is helping those who have been through divorce. I know how you're feeling. I strongly believe that the reason God hates divorce is because it's not just about husbands and wives splitting up. It divides whole families. We live in an instant society, and people don't always think things through before blindly jumping in. Giving up when situations become hard is the norm. God already gave us the working model for the family. When we do things our own way, that's when the enemy can come in. Children get their identity from their father whether he is present or absent. Mothers, please don't tear down the father of your children. When you tear him down, you also tear them down. Protect and cover your family in prayer. Teach them about Jesus and teach them how to pray. Be the example you want them to be.

I am fortunate, at my age, that both of my parents are still living. I love them right where they are. The reason I can is because of my relationship with Jesus. I had to answer this very important question: "Do I want to be right, or do I want a relationship with my parents?" I decided that I wanted a relationship with my parents. So, everything I was holding onto, I *let go*. You cannot grow walking in unforgiveness. Forgiveness is a requirement for salvation, so choose life.

As I grow older, I have found that nothing is more important than family. I love my parents dearly. Sometimes when I call my father, I say, "I don't want anything. I just wanted to say I love you and I was thinking about you." He responds, "I love you too, baby." It makes me smile thinking about it. If we both have time, we talk. If not, we save it for another day. The most freeing day of my life was when I released my father from my judgement and allowed him to just be my father. My heart opened and, from that day until now, I can receive the benefits of his love. It also helps me receive more of my heavenly Father's love, grace and mercy—for nothing is ever wasted when you use it for the Kingdom.

For more information about Genoa and her fearless way of life, visit www.GenoaPeak.online.

SELF-REFLECTION QUESTIONS

1. Why do you think divorce is so prevalent in today's society? Is unforgiveness a contributing factor in divorce?

   _____

   _____

   _____

   _____

   _____

   _____

2. How do our premarital choices impact the success or failures in marriage?

   _____

   _____

   _____

   _____

   _____

   _____

SELF-REFLECTION QUESTIONS

3. As believers, we have a role in the lives of children whose parents are going through divorce. What should our role be when we see the children being impacted negatively as a result of the divide?

_____

_____

_____

_____

_____

_____

4. How is Genoa able to forgive? Should forgiveness be optional for the victim?

_____

_____

_____

_____

_____

_____

Chapter 7

The Stranger
I Longed to Know

Tenita Johnson

*"Have I not commanded you? Be strong and courageous. Do not be
afraid; do not be discouraged, for the Lord your God will be with you
wherever you go."*

Joshua 1:9, New International Version

For many fatherless daughters, their life stories are centered around the men who left when they were young. The men who divorced their mothers and, consequently, divorced them. The men who called every now and then, and dropped a birthday gift off every other year. The men who showed up at their Kindergarten graduations, only to not show up again until high school graduation. I would have loved to enjoy any small fraction of those monumental events that a father should share with his daughter. But, my father was absent long before I had the chance to know he was missing from my life. I came into the world *fatherless*.

My father was absent long before I had the chance to know he was missing.

My mother gave birth to me at the age of fourteen, right before she entered her freshman year of high school. So, when I was born, we stayed in a one-bedroom apartment with my grandmother and grandfather. After all, my mother wasn't old enough to move out on her own. Many of my family members tell me I was my grandfather's favorite grandchild. Unfortunately, I don't remember him much at all. He passed away by the time I was four years old, leaving no one to guide me in a fatherly way. My mother is the youngest child of ten siblings. So, by the time I came along, all of my aunts and uncles lived outside the home. While I saw my aunts and uncles from time to time, my grandmother was my main guardian. My grandmother took me to school, the laundromat and church. Church. The place where I watched my grandmother serve on the ushers' board and the mothers' board, as well as the kitchen Sunday after Sunday. I was baptized when I was seven years old at my grandmother's home church, but at the time, I didn't even know what that meant. All I knew was I'd gotten wet by someone who held me under water for much too long, in my opinion.

I didn't know what I was missing. But I knew something, *someone* was missing. I made up stories about my father in elementary school when friends asked about my dad. It was hard only knowing a mom that did the best she could, and a grandmother that played the role of 'dad' the best she knew how. I always heard other kids talk about their mom *and* dad, while I tried not to talk about either for fear of people asking too many questions. I didn't understand why it was such a big secret that I didn't know my father. After all, I wasn't ashamed of the fact that I had never met him. But, it was apparently shameful for my mother. If anything, when people found out that I'd never met my biological father, it would have made them feel sorry for me. But I wasn't looking for sympathy. I wasn't looking for an apology from a classmate or teacher. I was looking for a *father*. And if the "I'm sorry" wasn't going to come from the horse's mouth, it wasn't going to do me any good.

I always thought life would have been *better* had I known my father. Maybe I would have had more clothes and shoes, which my cousins always teased me about not having. Maybe I could have gotten those $100 gym shoes from Foot Locker. Had I had all of this, the kids at school couldn't have possibly teased me about my nappy hair and dark skin. I daydreamed about my father picking me up from school; about him coming to my parent-teacher conferences; about him buying me a Bomb Pop off the local ice cream truck, but he never called. He never wrote. He never mysteriously appeared at school to pick me up. What happened that could cause this man to choose to have nothing at all to do with his own daughter?

Many times, when I asked my mother about my father, she immediately became angry. Her response was oftentimes, "You're not missing anything. You have a good life. There isn't anything that you lack by not knowing your father." But, like any curious child, I wanted the chance to make that decision for myself. Whenever I became angry with my mother or my grandmother, my immediate response was, "I wish I lived with my dad." I didn't know what he was like. I didn't know if he had a wife and other children. I didn't know if he lived in the hood or the hills. All I knew was that knowing him, living with him, had to be better than living with my mother and grandmother.

By the time I was twelve, my mother told me his name. Finally, she gave me a piece of the puzzle I'd been looking for. She told me that the last she'd heard, he'd moved to another state, was married with children and serving as the pastor of a church. But after several attempts at private investigations and unsuccessful cold phone calls, I still came up empty. I was looking for a father that did not seem to exist. Even though I knew of God, I still didn't know God. He was the God of my grandmother. And from what

After several attempts at private investigations and unsuccessful cold phone calls, I still came up empty.

I could see, she didn't have much victory and we surely didn't live the abundant life. Church was something we did, a weekly ritual more than

anything. But, the church wasn't in us. I was looking for evidence of what God had done because it would prove that He could do the same for me, but I still came up short.

As I progressed through life, it seemed like I was the only person in the entire world who had never met their biological father. But, we all know the enemy has a way of making us feel singled out in the crowd. Friends thought I was exaggerating about the whole situation for attention. It seemed impossible to them that a person could grow up, knowing absolutely nothing about one of their biological parents. Through the years, the words, "Your daddy didn't want you" and "You're a bastard child" continued to ring in my mind. It wasn't that people had said these words directly to me, but I had heard these phrases used before toward other people who didn't have a father in the home. And unfortunately, those were the people I most closely related to.

Call Off the Search

"A father to the fatherless, a defender of widows, is God in His holy habitation."

Psalm 68:5, English Standard Version

Even though my biological father was absent, I was fortunate enough to have many father figures who attempted to fill the void. I think I gave the word 'dad' a new meaning when I started using it for everyone in my life who treated me like I was their own. There were 'dads' who gave me extravagant birthday and Christmas gifts, such as the new pair of purple

Patrick Ewing gym shoes and the original Nintendo System. There was a 'dad' who helped pay my tuition to a Catholic elementary school so that I could have a better education than what was offered by the Chicago Public School system. There was a 'dad' who sent me money to match what I had saved toward the purchase of my first car. There was a 'dad' who made sure I got to high school every morning. That same 'dad' was there to cheer me on in my track and cross country meets when my mom couldn't make them. There was even a 'dad' who took the time to chastise me with a cutting board for skipping school. And I couldn't say, "You ain't my daddy" because, at that time, *he was*. There were 'dads' who I could talk to about issues that I seemed to think my mother just couldn't understand. But even with all of those people in my life, those 'dads' who made my life just a little bit smoother, there was still an empty space.

Even with all of those people in my life, there was still an empty space.

After years of searching and searching for my biological father, I reached a breaking point. I was tired of the unknown. In 2007, I attended a church service that would redirect my life forever. My pastor declared the year to be "The Year of Release". He instructed the entire congregation to take note cards and write down seven things we wanted God to do for us that year. We then laid the cards on the altar and my pastor said a corporate prayer over them. I don't remember all seven things that I wrote down, but I do remember writing down that I wanted to meet my biological father within that year. I was tired of sitting through Father's Day sermons, wondering where mine might be on that special day designated just for him. I was tired of being in that 'fatherless' prayer line every Father's Day. I had faith that God was going to let me meet him for the first time before midnight December 31, 2007. I sat through the New Year's Eve illustrated sermon, waiting on God to give me an answer or an explanation. God had done all of the things on my 'release' list, except that one. I was waiting in anticipation for a mysterious man to walk up to me in the middle of service and introduce himself as my father, but none of that happened.

All that was on my mind was meeting my father. I didn't understand why God wouldn't honor this one request. It wasn't until January of 2008 that God gave me a revelation. My pastor charged us to once again write seven things we wanted God to do for us in 2008. But he also said, "If God didn't answer all of your seven things on the list from last year, it either wasn't in His will or you don't need it." It was at that moment that I stopped searching. I was released from the stronghold of the unknown. God was leading me down a new path. I was finally ready to accept 'moving on'. But, nothing could prepare me for what would come eight years down the road.

The man who moved me into college, the man I knew as 'dad', had been a part of my life since I was thirteen. Although he and my mother never married, and they ended their relationship after irreconcilable differences, he remained in my life. He didn't let the fact that, because he and my mother were no longer together, come between our relationship. After all, he was the only father I knew for most of my teenage years. He was there when I graduated college. He was there when I got married (although my uncle gave me away). He was at the hospital for the birth of my children. And for many years, I didn't have to worry about Christmas shopping because he bought more for my children than my husband and I did. When I started publishing books, he was the first to buy not only

I didn't have a biological father, but I had a dad that more than qualified.

his copy, but ten more copies to share with his friends and family. I was his daughter. While I called him Edward when I was a teen, as I grew and acquired my own family, I grew to love him more and started calling him *Dad*. He was young in spirit and young at heart. I didn't have a biological father, but I had a dad that more than qualified. God gave me what I needed—until one morning when I woke up to a call at 6 a.m.

I spent a week going back and forth to the hospital after he'd suffered a heart attack. While he'd awakened on day two of his extended stay, days three and four were followed by nothing but a medicated comatose state. Every now and then, he'd move around in the bed to reposition himself, without opening his eyes, of course. He couldn't speak for the ventilator down his throat. On day two, I had hope. I knew it may take some time, but he was going to get better and come out just fine. We'd have to change his eating habits, and he may have needed a home health aide, but he was going to be fine. But by day seven, our worst nightmare had come true. In my head, I told myself, "I'm scared to let him go. I need him. I can't get through the rest of my life without him." After all, girls need their dads. Sure, I have a husband and male cousins, and many male friends I consider to be brothers, but none of them amounted to my dad. But in my moment of fear, in my moment of feeling unequipped, unqualified and uncomfortable, a still small voice said to me: "He's given you everything you need. You have everything you need to move forward."

And, in that moment, as I sat in a hallway with my sister on a window sill, waiting for the doctors to confirm what we already knew, I gave myself permission to move forward. For me. For dad. For everything he taught me and the things he left for me to figure out on my own. Because when your biggest fan dies, you've got to be able to cheer yourself on to the finish line. I was not his biological daughter, and my mother never married him, so I was not allowed to have my name printed in the obituary or on any of the legal documents regarding his death. It was one more reminder that he was borrowed, loaned out to me only for a season. He wasn't my father and I wasn't biologically his daughter. I wasn't entitled to anything. Once again, I was *fatherless*.

So, I thought.

Over the next few months, there were many days I felt like I would literally faint. I could be driving down the street and my legs would go numb or feel like they were buckling under me. In the Word, 2 Corinthians 12:10 (New American Standard Bible) says, *"Therefore I am well content with weaknesses, with insults, with distresses, with persecutions, with difficulties, for Christ's sake; for when I am weak, then I am strong."* It was only through God's loving grace and mercy that I made it through this trying time. I found a strength I'd never known, a strength I never *needed* to know—until now. Even though I was married with my own children, I still depended on my father a lot. But, God showed me that I should only put my hope and trust in Him. Everything and everyone else is temporal. God is eternal. Again, I knew of God, but I'd never had to trust Him like I trusted my dad because, well, I had my dad. It

I've never been fatherless. My heavenly Father has been with me every step of the way.

was like the rug of security was pulled from under me and God, and only God, could comfort me. Little did I know, God was *more* than enough. I pressed my way into a new level of prayer, a new level of worship, a new trust in the Most High God. I'd heard He could heal every manner of sickness and disease, heartbreak and heartache. But I needed to experience the authentic healing power of God for myself. It's only been a little over two years, and I'd be lying if I said the healing process is complete. It's more like a day-to-day journey that simply gets easier with time and prayer. While I miss the man I knew as my father, the truth of the matter is, I've never been fatherless. My heavenly Father has been with me every step of the way—and He hasn't failed me or left me yet.

Favored and Fearless

"And my God will liberally supply (fill until full) your every need according to His riches in glory in Christ Jesus."

Philippians 4:19, Amplified Bible

God had already prepared me for success by putting spiritual fathers in place of my biological father. Through the grace of God, I was an honor roll student and I graduated at the top of my high school class. I graduated from college with a Bachelor of Journalism, as well as with a Master of Marketing from graduate school. But that was just the tip of the iceberg. There was so much more lying dormant on the inside of me that I knew not of. In December of 2015, my late pastor, Bishop Ben Gibert, spoke a word over the house that struck a chord in me. He said, "God is opening big doors for you! Doors you didn't pray for. Doors you didn't knock on. But for His name's sake and for His glory, He's taking you places man could have never taken you. This is going to be *big*!"

Since that day, I've been speaking and declaring, "God's opening big doors for His people!" The message never gets stale. It never gets old. I still believe it. I still use it to encourage others. On social media, people even tag me in pictures of large doors, colorful doors, and unique, extraordinary doors. Doors signify both the beginning and the end of a thing. As we walk through the door, we often walk out of something into something else—another room, another area, another level. So, while I shut the door on depression, sadness and self-doubt because I've never met my biological father—and I may never—I choose to walk through doors of encouragement, motivation, inspiration and prosperity. I don't wear the "fatherless daughter" tag as a badge of honor or sorrow. As a matter of fact, I won't even mention it unless I'm in a setting where that part of my story is relevant, which isn't often. I'm too focused on the big doors that God is continuously opening in my life to focus on the small ones that He has closed.

Today, one of the big doors we're holding open is bringing marriages back together. My husband and I spend a significant amount of time serving married couples in and outside the four walls of the church. Even though we both grew up in households without a father present, we're on a mission to end the ever-increasing epidemic of divorce in the home, which often leads to broken families and fatherless children. Also, as a full-time entrepreneur, author and speaker, I continue to walk through the big doors God continues to open. I have the honor of helping people transform the world through words through my company, *So It Is Written Writing & Editing Services, LLC.* In addition to helping people tell their story in excellence, I help entrepreneurs and authorpreneurs alike establish their brand in a unique, creative way that'll help them stand out amongst the competition in the marketplace. As a six-time published author, I've visualized myself speaking on stages

These things are just the appetizers to the main course God has in store for me.

around the world, empowering others to not only walk in their truth—but to *write it.* In 2017, my book, *When the Smoke Clears: A Phoenix Rises,* was adapted into a stage play, which ran for one weekend in downtown Detroit to three sold-out audiences. In addition, I host The Red Ink Conference for Authors & Editors annually in two cities around the nation, serving as a catalyst of change for authors and editorial professionals worldwide. To the world, my plate may seem full, but I know these things are just the appetizers to the main course God has in store for me.

I'd be lying if I said I don't miss the man I knew as dad. I'd be lying if I said I didn't think about who or where my biological father is. But what God has continually shown me over and over again is that He, and He alone, is more than enough. I learned early in the healing process that brokenness is a critical step. In our brokenness, in our authenticity and vulnerability, is where God meets us and rebuilds us. He picks us up, dusts us off and shows us that, in Him, we're worth much more than this world could ever give us. I no longer search for what could have been or what should have been. I know now that my identity—which I once saw as so very broken—can only be whole, validated and fulfilled through Christ Jesus.

For more information about Tenita and her fearless way of life, visit www.SoItIsWritten.net.

SELF-REFLECTION QUESTIONS

1. If you could say or ask your biological father one thing, what would it be?

    _____

    _____

    _____

    _____

    _____

    _____

2. How would your life have been different if your father was more involved in your life?

    _____

    _____

    _____

    _____

    _____

    _____

SELF-REFLECTION QUESTIONS

3. How was your relationship with God affected by the absence of your father?

   _____

   _____

   _____

   _____

   _____

   _____

   _____

4. Make a list of seven things you need to forgive your father for. Pray them aloud daily.

   _____

   _____

   _____

   _____

   _____

   _____

   _____

Chapter 8

Bruised,
but not Broken

Jamie Hopkins

*"He that dwelleth in the secret place of the most High shall abide under the
shadow of the Almighty."*

Psalm 91:1, King James Version

My first impression of a man was my father. His lack of affection and unforgiveness led me down the same path. It seemed like he only cared about watching wrestling on TV and drinking. He was an alcoholic, so I really couldn't tell if he was just angry at us, or angry at life in general. He wasn't a very expressive man, other than when he was angry. He spanked us with everything from wooden boards to skinny tree branches. Every spanking, which often left us with long scars on our bodies, also left us unable to sit down. But that was nothing compared to how he treated my mom. He physically abused her so frequently that it became the norm in our household. I was four years old when I first saw my father violently put his hands on my mother. He beat her as if he was a football player who was ready to pick off his opponent. After years of my father's abuse, my mother finally got the courage to pack up and leave.

Every spanking, which often left us with long scars on our bodies, also left us unable to sit down.

I started going to church at a very young age. Every Sunday my mother dropped me and my sisters off at Sunday School, and she would later join us at the regular church service. My family was full of devout believers in God, and they made sure they passed along the tradition of going to church every Sunday to their children. Truth be told, it was our faith in God that kept us from what happened next. Even though we entered the Lord's house every week, no one ever knew what was happening in our house behind closed doors.

By the time I was five years old, I had my second encounter with a man. I was sexually abused by my uncle. As a kid, I thought that what my uncle did to me was normal and that every family experienced the same thing. Besides, kids follow what the adults do. We're only sponges who repeat the same patterns. I was a clear product of my environment. The women in my family didn't fight back or even talk about the level of abuse that was happening in our family. I never talked about the sexual abuse either. I did as I was told and kept silent. My relatives also upheld the family tradition of silencing the victim. My family firmly believed in the old adage, "You don't talk about what goes on in your home."

Even though my mom remarried, our family dynamic went from bad to worse. My mom's second husband was the evilest man I ever met. He was not only physically abusive, but he was verbally abusive too. He was so bad that I often wondered why my mom didn't just stay with my dad. At least he wasn't as bad as this man. Her new husband came home every weekend, completely wasted. He'd force my mom into the car and drive off to God knows where. When they returned, my mom's face would be covered in blood. He beat the crap out of her. When it got really bad, she would call my name. Many times I got out of bed and jumped on his back, in defense of my mom. He then, in turn, beat me. I was okay with it as long as he wasn't hitting my mom. I was a young teenager, and this was my third encounter with a man. By this time, I didn't trust men at all. I saw them as angry, weak, evil human beings.

I often asked myself, *"When will I ever wake up from this nightmare?"* It seemed like the drama would never end. At the age of 17, my mom enlisted me in the U.S. Navy. I felt guilty for leaving my mom and sisters in that abusive environment, but it was my intent to find a way to rescue them. Little did I know that my path ahead would be an extremely painful one, as I discovered how to heal from fatherlessness and the abuse of my childhood.

I had a baby girl a year after joining the Navy. I bought my first car, joined a local church and met my soon-to-be husband. Though I carried the pain of my childhood everywhere I went, I tried to make the most of my life. Yet, I was still miserable. I cried constantly behind closed doors because I felt hopeless and unlovable. I didn't know where these feelings were coming from. I'd built a happy, prosperous life for me and my daughter. One day, it all came to the forefront. It was the darkest demon ever to live in the corners of my soul. The one thing I could no longer ignore or escape. *My past.*

I was 28 years old when my past decided to haunt me and ruin my perfect life. I was married to a man who was a good father to my child. I had also become a stepmom of his three kids. We were a true blended family. I didn't really know them and they didn't know me. Honestly, at that time, *I didn't even know me.* Everyone only knew what I portrayed on the outside, the me that I convinced myself that I was because the *real me* was broken.

My husband didn't realize I was a mess. He inherited a heart that had been damaged so badly, I thought it was irreparable. But it was my marriage and my husband that forced me to face my

A past that, if ever revealed, would change my life and the lives of my family forever.

ugly, dark, deepest secret of my past. A past that, if ever revealed, would change my life and the lives of my family forever. A past that took me years to speak out loud about. Every time I tell the story, it's uncomfortable. I never know how people will perceive it or perceive *me*. It's my past. It's my makeup. It's my truth.

So, there I was in my late 20's, newly married to a minister. I was a mother of a blended family of four, yet broken from my past. My fatherless story mirrored that of many fatherless daughters: abandonment issues, not trusting men, low self-esteem, depression, anxiety, suicidal ideation and a perfect mask to hide it all. Underneath that mask, I was completely unhappy. There was nothing anyone could do because no one knew my secret. I played the happy wife and mother well in front of the church, just like I was raised to do by many other women who kept their ugly truths inside. As soon as my past reared its ugly head, I left my husband. I left my faith. I left everything I thought I knew and loved because I didn't know what was real. I didn't know what was right. I literally lost my mind. I lost all sense of reality. I was in so much emotional pain that I could hardly breathe. There was no way I could be a wife or a mother to someone else's kids when I didn't even want to be a mother to my own child. I couldn't escape my daughter, so she would have to come along for the nightmare of a ride. I was officially a single mother again, accompanied by the pain that continued to rock my soul.

Breaking Bad

"Come to Me, all you who labor and are heavy laden and I will give you rest."

Matthew 11:28, New King James Version

I was going downhill, *fast*. Four years after divorcing my husband and leaving the church, I started taking prescription drugs to ease the pain of my past. After a while, the pain pills weren't enough. So, I drank profusely and slept around, with no conscience of contracting sexually transmitted diseases or falling in love. I ignored all the signs of safety and took dangerous risks with my life. I didn't care if I lived or died. But, to get rid of the pain, I wanted to die. I even tried to take my own life.

One lonely night in my one-bedroom apartment, my daughter was sleeping peacefully on the living room couch. I sat on the bathroom floor with a knife resting on my wrist. My eyes were swollen red from crying hysterically, while negative

I sat on the bathroom floor with a knife resting on my wrist.

and hopeless thoughts rushed through my head. I thought about how I would never be happy again. I thought about how I was so messed up that no one could ever truly love me. I was ready to end it all. I pressed hard on the knife because I wanted to bleed out on my bathroom floor. Then, my daughter moved and made a sound. I thought about her finding me lifeless on the bathroom floor. Who was going to take care of her? Who was going to put her broken pieces back together after finding her mother covered in blood on the bathroom floor? Tears flooded my eyes even more. I couldn't put my daughter through that pain. I picked myself up off that bathroom floor, got in my bed and cried myself to sleep.

I had lived this tormented life for such a long time that I gave up hope that God loved me. I was angry with God for allowing my life to be cursed, and for allowing my entire family to be cursed. The level of abuse that is so rampant in my family is appalling, and God did absolutely nothing to stop it. We were babies. We were helpless. How could He allow this to happen to babies? I was confused and I was angry. But most of all, I was hurt. Bruised very badly. I needed someone to blame, so I blamed God.

My reckless living carried on for ten years. Looking back now, I shake my head in *awe* that God kept me through all of it – the drug and alcohol abuse, the sexually transmitted diseases that were curable, and the smoking. Despite the thousands and thousands of pills I swallowed on a regular basis, God kept me. The numbing sensation from the pills was just a temporary fix, because every time I closed my eyes at night there was a monster in the corner of my bedroom, waiting to pounce on my chest and suffocate me. I was tormented by my past. Every. Single. Night.

My emotional healing journey began when I had a monumental breakthrough in therapy. Even though I told myself I was angry with God, I intentionally searched for a Christian-based therapist. Proverbs 22:6 (King James Version) says, *"Train up a child in the way he should go: and when he is old, he will not depart from it."* My family made sure we attended church regularly. My faith, even though I rejected it outwardly, was still intact and working in mysterious ways.

In my first therapy session, I said two things: "I'm angry with God, so don't give me any Biblical principles or church clichés because that won't work for me. And give me a date when all of this pain will be over!" To this day, both my therapist and I laugh at our first appointment together. She knew

I'm angry with God, so don't give me any Biblical principles or church clichés because that won't work for me.

from day one that I would be a handful! And I was. She was so patient with me, and she completely disregarded my first rule by ending every session with a Scripture. She allowed me to express all of my anger. She also allowed me to cry out all of my pain. This helped me to release my aggression, doubts, fears and worries. It was like putting a Band-Aid over a sore. That Band-Aid protected the sore from being damaged any further while it was in the healing phase. That Band-Aid was God's Word. The day I walked into my therapist's office was the day my life completely changed.

Made Brand New

"No weapon that is formed against thee shall prosper; and every tongue that shall rise against thee in judgment thou shalt condemn. This is the heritage of the servants of the Lord, and their righteousness is of me, saith the Lord."

Isaiah 54:17, King James Version

When you've been in pain as long as I have, you begin to lose faith and hope that things will get better. You begin to think and believe that this (pain) is all there is to your life. It seems like you're cursed and the only way out is

121

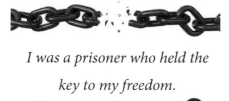

I was a prisoner who held the key to my freedom.

death. When someone comes along and tries to give you a different outlook on life, you are not convinced. Your pain has become a resting place in your soul because it's all you know and believe. Peace, to you, is an unobtainable goal.

Peace, for me, came around just like my biological father did—every now and then. I feared the unknown. I wasn't willing to take that step, that risk of faith, to become free. Fear kept me stuck in my dark and dreadful past. I was a prisoner who held the key to my freedom, but I was too afraid to use it to unlock the door. I had that key all along. I just didn't know how to use it.

When I started to get weary on my emotional healing journey, I had a vision. Imagine this: God is busy at work in His wood shop. He sits at this wooden table with thousands of broken little pieces spread out in front of Him. It looks like a puzzle, but God is not concerned about those thousands of broken pieces. He patiently sits there, putting the pieces back together. He picks up one piece, holds it close to His eyes, examines it closely, then says, "Doubt... no, not here." He tosses the broken piece to the floor, then grabs another one. He continues this process of elimination until He has formed the perfect masterpiece in front of Him. When complete, He sits back, crosses His arms, and marvels at the beautiful sculpture before Him. He calls for His Son in the other room, "Jesus, come see this!"

Jesus comes in the room and stands next to His Father, gazing upon the well-crafted sculpture on the wood table. They both seem oblivious to the mess of broken pieces on the floor surrounding them. They are solely focused on the beautiful masterpiece on the table. Jesus shakes His head in awe, "You did it again!" God smiles at the sculpture and says proudly, "This is Jai. She will be the voice of that child crying out in the dark. She will carry the torch for the hurt to be healed."

God took my broken pieces and made me whole again. He took all the doubt, fears, insecurities, hurt, pain, agony, hate, anger, bitterness, deceit, betrayal, abortions, financial hardships, worrying, homelessness, bad relationships, loneliness, confusion, depression, suicidal thoughts, bad decisions, ill-intentions, self-inflicted pain—and He made me whole again. He even changed my name! You see, I had been living in fear for a long time. Fear was the first cousin to my pain. I didn't see any other way out of my situation until God gave me a vision of hope. Through everything that ever happened, it was my faith that always returned in my darkest times.

Sometimes, the fear of the unknown is greater than the fear of freedom. That's until someone comes along that breeds happiness and healing. She was once an emotionally broken, fatherless daughter, but now she's whole. She has a glow around her and it looks like she is walking on air. Literally. She reaches out her hand for you to grab hold. She wants to pull you through those prison bars and free you from your painful, dreadful past. Will you take the journey less traveled?

For years, I searched for my father in every encounter I ever had with a man. Every encounter left me abandoned, neglected, empty and unloved. That was until I established my personal relationship with the Heavenly

Father. I had to open my heart to receive the truth of who God was to me in order to heal. The truth is that I've been hurt, bruised and mentally broken. But today, I am walking in my healing daily.

Even though I don't have a relationship with my biological father, I choose to rest in God's arms and walk in His purpose for my pain. Today, I am a certified victim's advocate. I've started two businesses under my company, *Matters of My Heart, LLC*. One entity is an emotional support mentoring program for adult survivors of childhood domestic and sexual abuse. The other entity is a self-publishing company for aspiring authors who are ready to tell their story and be healed from their past. My passion is to help survivors of abuse transition from a place of hurt to a place of emotional healing, providing them with practical self-care and self-help tools along the journey. I've traveled the world, studied many different philosophies, produced a radio show for two years, written six books, went back to college and obtained two master's degrees in Business Management. I use every opportunity to share my story to help others heal, and I'm just getting started!

Your past doesn't define you; it refines you.

Your past doesn't define you; it refines you. There is life after pain and there is purpose to your suffering. Seek that safe place to release the pain so you can be free to live on purpose, with purpose. I'll close with the same Scripture I started with because this has carried me through the darkest of dark times. Psalm 91:1 (King James Version) says, *"He that dwelleth in the secret place of the Most High shall abide under the shadow of the Almighty."*

For more information about Jamie and her fearless way of life, visit www.MattersOfMyHeart.com.

SELF-REFLECTION QUESTIONS

1. What secret(s) are you keeping inside that you're too afraid to share with someone else?

_____

_____

_____

_____

_____

_____

2. When you look in the mirror, what do you see?

_____

_____

_____

_____

_____

_____

_____

SELF-REFLECTION QUESTIONS

3. How do you cope with your emotional pain?

_____

_____

_____

_____

_____

_____

_____

4. Do you have a support system and self-care regimen in place to cope with your emotional pain? If not, why not? What is preventing you from getting one?

_____

_____

_____

_____

_____

_____

_____

Guiding Your Way Through

Candice Crear

"For many are called, but few are chosen."

Matthew 22:14, English Standard Version

It's been a while since I wrote my first book, *Invisible Dad*, the international best-seller and International Book Award Finalist that shook the hearts of the fatherless. It not only exposed the truth of a painful epidemic, but it gave others the freedom to do the same. As I was writing the book, I didn't know what would happen with my heart-felt work, let alone if anyone would read it. My focus was to obey the direction that God gave me and to complete my healing process once and for all. And that's what I did. I did the work, and God opened many other paths along the way. The aftermath of the obedience has truly blown my mind, but I had to focus on what God told me.

By the end of 2015, my purpose was unveiled. God revealed to me that I was going to bring His daughters back to Him, but I wasn't sure how He wanted me to do that. I saw many nonprofit organizations helping children reunite with their fathers and providing male mentors. I also saw many fatherhood organizations teaching men the skillset to raise their children effectively. The gaping hole was the lack of support for fatherless women. If we, as a nation, are going to stop this epidemic, we must approach it from all fronts. After being a guest on various radio and talk shows, attending events, and further researching the *new normal* of being fatherless, it became more obvious that I was supposed to coach fatherless women. God called me for more than authoring a book. He called me to conquer the road less traveled: to be a coach and teacher for fatherless women.

Per the United States Census, 24.7 million children don't live with their biological father. As the fatherless children grow up, the statistics get worse. Children are four times more likely to be poor if their father is not around

24.7 million children don't live with their biological father.

(National Public Radio). Fatherless daughters are four times more likely to get pregnant as teenagers (National Survey of Family Growth), and 85% of all children who show behavioral disorders come from fatherless homes (Center of Disease Control). With women passing on their broken nature to their children, this epidemic is spreading like wildfire. To end this dreadful sweep of abandonment, my focus is to teach women how to heal and take responsibility for their own lives. In turn, they'll be able to care for themselves and their children with stability, confidence and hope for a better tomorrow.

Being a guide through the healing process is effortless for me because I've lived through it. The healing phases in *Invisible Dad* are the roadmap to being fearless, but there is nothing like having someone with you that can take you through the process and lead you to the finish line. I'd love to tell you that I stepped all in with confidence, but it didn't quite start that way. I was looking for examples of others that actually did what I was called to do, but I came up short. God was calling me to do something *different*. I was created to be purposefully *uncommon*. Once I owned my calling and stepped all the way in, God started to use me to my fullest extent. The bravest part is that I never looked back.

Now, I sit here in a hotel room, telling you that I am starting a movement–a *From Fatherless to Fearless* movement. All of the speaking engagements, coaching calls, live interviews and classes I've taught have all led up to this moment. As a victim of fatherlessness, I know the fear of abandonment and rejection overtakes you. It's my purpose to help you conquer life, business and the pursuit of happiness by moving you through the healing process. You will

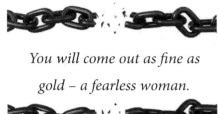

You will come out as fine as gold – a fearless woman.

come out as fine as gold – a fearless woman – one who is ready to walk in her calling and embrace her story. I am here to help you with the 'to' on your path to healing. My passion is to see fatherless women come out of the darkness as beautiful roses in full bloom. Are you ready to go *From Fatherless to Fearless?*

Stages of a Fatherless Woman

"Your greatest test is in how you handle the person you hate."

Bishop T.D. Jakes

By now, you've read the beautiful stories of eight women who've conquered their paths to fearlessness. The journey is not easy. It took me almost ten years to completely heal. In today's society, women have learned to cope by waving the flag of independence instead of facing the truth head on. It's okay to be independent, but emasculating men to make yourself feel better further adds to the tragedy. My challenge to all fatherless women is to focus on healing, and to be the best *you* that you can be. Let God handle the rest.

In order to heal, you first need to know the healing stages of a fatherless woman. When you can identify where you are, you can take the necessary steps to get where you want to be. These four stages will help you navigate your healing journey and pinpoint your focus:

1. Denial

Let's face it. You're still in denial that being fatherless is even affecting you. But acting like it doesn't exist doesn't mean the pain isn't there. You look strong on the outside, but you break down when no one is looking. You don't even realize that you're angry all the time. You either hate all men, or you may latch onto them and forget all of your morals. The fact that you're a fatherless daughter is not your fault, but it's time to take responsibility for the choices you make in life so you can move forward.

Primary Focus:

"In Him we have redemption through His blood, the forgiveness of sins, according to the riches of His grace..."

Ephesians 1:7, New King James Version

It's time to face your truth head on. Nothing changes if nothing changes. Take the first step by understanding who Jesus Christ is for *yourself.* He knew what you would do before you did it, yet He still died for you. This same redemptive love is given to your father. When you let go, you'll come to the realization that by opening yourself to Jesus, you cut the chains from your own ankles.

2. Stagnant

You know something isn't right, but you're not sure where to turn to fix it. You're having continuous problems in your relationships, especially with those in authority and those in your love life. It's the battle of 'who's the boss'. You blame your father for almost everything in your past, present and future. You've heard the term *forgiveness* over and over again, but you don't feel you should forgive anyone because you've done nothing wrong.

Primary Focus:

"Bear with each other and forgive one another if any of you has a grievance against someone. Forgive as the Lord forgave you."

Colossians 3:13, New International Version

Take the time to understand what forgiveness truly means. It's the hardest road to conquer when it comes to fatherlessness. The misconception of forgiveness is that it's optional. This is far from the truth. In order to overcome the cards you've been dealt, forgiveness is *required*. God is not saying it never happened; He's telling you to stop pointing the finger at someone else so you can work on yourself. If you want the true definition of freedom, forgiveness sums it up.

3. In the Fire

Congratulations! You've started your healing journey. You realized there was a problem, and you took action to try and solve it. The healing process leaves you feeling vulnerable and broken. It's like all you ever knew is being washed away before your eyes. In the midst of this great exchange (Isaiah 61:3), you are pushing to stay in the fight. There are ways you thought were right, but God is showing you a new path. You feel lost, but know that this is the right place to be.

Primary Focus:

"And after you have suffered a little while, the God of all grace, who has called you to his eternal glory in Christ, will himself restore, confirm, strengthen, and establish you."

1 Peter 5:10, English Standard Version

Trust God to put you back together better than ever before. Allow Him to restore you. Soon, you'll be on the other side of the mountain and I encourage you to never look back. Focus on the beauty of the end. God is making you a new person, so have patience in the process. You'll need to learn and unlearn some things, but trust that He is with you the entire way.

4. Living in Your Testimony

You did it! Although healing is a continuous journey, you're through the hardest part. You've gone through the phases of *redemption, forgiveness* and *restoration*. Now, you're ready to share your story of what God has done. First, you have to release the need for perfection. Exposing yourself leaves you worried about what others may say.

Primary Focus:

"Fear not, for I am with you; be not dismayed, for I am your God;
I will strengthen you, I will help you, I will uphold you with my
righteous right hand."

Isaiah 41:10, English Standard Version

Break out and be fearless! God didn't bring you out of this turmoil for you to sit in silence. Be bold and courageous, and share your testimony with others. Having confidence in God gets you through the moments when you feel less than adequate. When we share our testimony, it puts one more nail in the coffin of defeat. You know exactly what other fatherless women are going through. Help them through the process of healing.

The four stages of a fatherless woman – Denial, Stagnant, In the Fire and Living in Your Testimony – are imperative to your success. At some point, you'll need to go through all four stages to reach your fearless ending. I've made it easy for you to understand what stage you're in. Visit

At some point, you'll need to go through all four stages to reach your fearless ending.

www.FromFatherlessToFearless.com to take the *From Fatherless to Fearless* quiz. After you answer a few questions, you'll know exactly what stage you're in and how to take your next step toward being your best self.

I'm excited about your journey. I know what it takes, but I also know what you'll get in return. God will not fail you. Everything you've gone through is refining you into something greater, something more, something worth it.

Support for Your Journey

"If you want something, you have to release your faith to get it."

Pastor Kym Lyons

We are all uniquely connected, with one mission: to be better than we were yesterday.

The best part about your healing journey is that you don't have to tread the mountain alone. God has sent me to guide you along the way. Plus, there's fatherless women around the world that are ready to support you. Join the *From Fatherless to Fearless* Facebook group, which I created as a safe haven for all of us to talk about our feelings and milestones. We are all uniquely connected, with one mission: to be better than we were yesterday.

With God as the foundation, and our faith as the anchor, we'll be able to transform our brokenness into a blessing. Just wait and see!

For more information on how to navigate your healing journey, visit www.FromFatherlessToFearless.com.

Made in the USA
Columbia, SC
07 March 2018